We Only Live Once

We Only Live Once

Memoir of a Survivor

Karine Tobin

We Only Live Once
Published by Karine Tobin 2019
Published with support by Author Express

First Edition 2019

Copyright © 2019 Karine Tobin

All rights reserved.

No part of this publication may be reproduced, stored in a retrieval system, or transmitted in any form or by any means, electronic, mechanical, photocopying, recording or otherwise, without the prior written permission from both the copyright owner and publisher.

Disclaimer:
Some names, places and identifying details have been changed to protect for privacy and maintain their anonymity. I may have changed some identifying characteristics and details such as physical properties, occupations and places of residence. This book contains cultural and indigenous references and language, for telling the story and is not meant to offend, or have any ill intent towards real life culture or indigenous people.

Every effort has been made to ensure that this book is free from error or omissions. However, the author, publisher, editor or their agents or representatives shall not accept responsibility for any loss or inconvenience caused to a person or organisation relying on this information.

A catalogue record for this book is available from the National Library of Australia

Title: We Only Live Once : Memoir of a survivor

ISBN:
9781925471465 Paperback
9781925471489 E-book

Illustrator: Tobin, Elyze
Cover designed and formatted by Self-Publishing Lab

Visit www.karinetobin.com

For my husband, my children, my family, and my best friends.
I love you all more than you'll ever know.
I hope this story will help you live more mindfully.
Take care of yourself, your health, and your loved ones.
They are what's important.
Nothing else really matters.
Karine

Introduction

Everyone has their own story. This book brings you along on my extensive journey of discovering that life should never be taken for granted. Every moment deserves to be lived to its fullest, because in the end, it helps you understand the big picture: that everything happens for a reason, even if it seems unfair or outrageous at times. Later on down the track, you will understand why it had to be that way, because what happens doesn't really matter. It's how you respond that does. I've also learned that health and time are worth more than riches, and I would give away all the money in the world to get more time with my family.

This book is for my children, Jack and Elyze, and my wonderful husband, Justin. I love them so much. Somewhere along the line, they saved my life, and I want them to have a reminder of it; something tangible they can keep forever. They are my reasons for living. They're part of me, and I want to be with them every day of their lives, sharing precious moments along the way. Even in my craziest and most beautiful dreams, I never could have imagined being blessed by such an amazing family. They are everything I've always wanted in the deepest recesses of my heart.

This is not only my story; it's our story. Because I didn't want them to struggle to read this in my native language, French, I've tried my best to write down my feelings and memories in English. Of course, I hope to be around long enough to tell this story myself, face to face, and also teach them their second language. But life can surprise you, so I prefer to be safe rather than sorry.

1

It's September 2015 in Sydney. I'm thirty weeks pregnant and definitely bigger than I was during my last pregnancy. My belly is already so big, I can't walk or see my feet. I'm like a giant bowling ball. I can't believe it. From now on, every day is a bonus for me, and I really hope this time around. I will carry this baby to term and leave the hospital with balloons and presents, like all the other mums.

Our first pregnancy started back in June 2013, a year and eight months into my marriage to Justin. I'd just done a pregnancy test, and it was positive. I was nearly in tears, so excited. Ecstatic, even. My twin sister, Laetitia, had just visited. She'd come all the way to Sydney from Paris to meet my husband and introduce us to her beautiful baby girl, Emy. I guess spending two weeks with such a cute one-year-old convinced us to have one of our own, and we started trying as soon as she left. A couple of months later, it finally happened. I'd been feeling sick and emotional for a week and wondering if I was pregnant. Laeti had been the first to know, of course. We'd done the test together over the phone.

I gave Justin a present that evening.

"What is it?" he asked. "Why do I have a present? It's not my birthday."

"Open it." I said, beaming with excitement.

He unwrapped the small package and discovered a small jar of baby food, an apple, and banana puree.

"Is that it? Is that what I believe it is?" he asked with tears in his eyes.

"Yes," I said.

I was so excited as I showed him the t-shirt I was wearing. There was a picture of an Anne Geddes baby, along with the positive pregnancy test. "You're going to be a daddy."

He was so happy. Tears formed in his eyes, and he brought me into his arms for a big cuddle. Then he kissed me with passion and bent over my belly to add, "You'll be a boy. You'll be a boy. Make a boy." It was funny. I love when he's happy, and he was over the moon. He took me back in his arms and held me tight.

I'd been smoking a couple of cigarettes a day back then, and I quit straight away. It's funny how easy it is to give up such a bad habit after so many years, once you're aware you have a human being growing inside you, even though it can be a weird feeling and scary at times.

I spent the next few weeks wondering if I needed to change my eating habits, sleep in a different position, stop my daily gym workouts, or if I should go private or public in terms of hospital care. Life was changing for the better, except that I was getting emotional. Justin and I were happily excited to become three. He helped me a lot at home, so I could rest, which gave me a nice feeling of support.

I wanted to keep it a secret from the outside world for the first three months, as nothing is really certain until then. Yet I did tell my parents, and we decided to tell Justin's mum. They were happy for us and promised not to tell anyone. Some of my workmates figured it out because of my "glow." Justin and I couldn't help but look at baby stuff and start thinking of our future family.

After eleven weeks, I had my first antenatal appointment. Justin came with me, and together we listened to the baby's heart. It was such a special moment. I was happy and laughing so hard, that we had to stop the foetal Doppler. The interferences with the machine were too noisy to listen to the beats. The nurse thought I was fifteen weeks pregnant rather than eleven, which was a bit comforting for me, as I'd put on nearly three kilos already. I still had to do the fourteen-week scan to make sure the baby's health was fine and rule out Down Syndrome, so the next day, Justin and I went back to the hospital to meet our baby for the first time.

We arrived at the radiology department and couldn't wait to enter the ultrasound room, not only because I'd drunk a lot of water, and my bladder was ready to explode, but also because we were longing to see our baby. After a little while, the technician led us into the room. I was excited and a bit nervous. I'd seen ultrasounds done in movies before, but now it was us. We were at the start of parenthood. We'd both decided not to know the gender, as Justin wanted it to be a surprise. We let the technician know not to tell us, but somehow, I thought it was a boy.

She started by putting some gel on my belly and then passed the monitor over it. Seeing our baby was so magical. Their little head, arms, and legs. I was nearly crying with happiness. But after a little while, I realised that the technician was quiet. I started to feel anxious and worried that something wasn't right. Then she left the room without a word to us.

"There's something wrong," I told Justin.

"No, you're worrying for nothing. She's going to come back. Everything is fine." He touched my hand, trying to comfort me.

"I'm telling you, she was too quiet. This is beautiful, and I was so excited to see the baby. She should have been happier, even if she's used to this. I'm scared something is happening. I don't know what it is, but there's a problem."

"Let's wait and see, okay?" he said. "Please calm down. We'll know more when she gets back." He rubbed at my shoulder to get the tension out.

At this point, the technician came back into the room and said with no emotion, "You need to talk to the doctor."

"Why? What's happening?" I asked.

"I can't explain it myself. You need to talk to the doctor. I'll show you the way now."

We followed her to the maternity ward, and she indicated a room where we could sit. The wait was excruciating. I felt a knot form in my chest, and as the minutes ticked on, Justin started worrying, too.

"See? I told you. Something's not right. Why else would we need to see the doctor? I'm so scared, Justin…" I said and began sobbing.

The doctor entered the room. She wore a surgical uniform, as if she'd just performed a delivery. An intern came in behind her.

"Hi… sorry, why are we here? What's happening with the baby?" I asked, urgency in my tone.

"Unfortunately, the baby's brain didn't develop," she said. "And they won't be able to grow properly if you pursue the pregnancy. It's a known condition called anencephaly."

The news was devastating. With just a few words, she'd ripped our hearts apart.

"What does it mean? I don't understand. What did I do wrong?"

I was in shock and crying so much, I could barely hear her answer.

"You didn't do anything wrong. It's a rare condition that happens to only one in ten thousand babies," she said, while offering me tissues. "In this case, the hospital can offer to promptly terminate the pregnancy. You can do it tomorrow, if it's convenient for you. Usually, the earlier, the better," she added, clearly feeling for us.

"Oh, my God. I can't believe this. One in ten thousand, and it happened to us."

Justin held me tight in his arms, barely coping with his own emotions. I thought about the ultrasound and how I'd been so happy, I hadn't seen that my baby's brain was missing. I'd just met them, and I had to say goodbye already. The tears wouldn't stop coming and were rolling down my cheeks. I was devastated. It was surreal. What had we done to deserve so much suffering?

The doctor said, "Sometimes it's a lack of folic acid, but you're taking supplements, so maybe it's not that. Or you should have taken a higher dose, as there isn't much in these tablets. But as I said, it's rare, and it's unfortunate, but there was nothing you could have done to really prevent it." Then she said, "Do you want me to leave you for a while?"

"No, that's fine. We'll come back tomorrow." I looked at Justin for approval.

"It's up to you, my love. Whatever you want," Justin said, grief clouding his face.

"Yes, it's pointless to wait any longer," I said. "What time should I come tomorrow?" I asked while trying to regain some kind of composure.

"Seven a.m. Here, at the maternity ward."

We left the hospital devastated, weakened, and heartbroken. All the happiness and excitement we'd had at the start of this appointment was taken away by the terrible news. Justin didn't cry. He was trying to show strength and support. At least one of us had to stay strong. We went for a coffee and had a quiet walk on our favourite beach at La Perouse. I was still pregnant, my baby moving in my belly, alive. For now.

I felt so guilty. I was the one carrying the child, after all. I figured maybe something was wrong with me. I started doubting that I could have a normal baby.

We went back home after renting a couple of movies. As always, we had our shower together, and that night the water covered our flooding tears while we both held my belly, giving our last goodbyes to our beautiful unborn soul.

"They're still alive. Still moving in me. I can't believe we have to abandon our child. This is so painful." I couldn't stop thinking about the innocent life I was about to take away. My first baby…our first baby. "We were so happy, and now this. It's too hard," I blurted.

"I'll try to be strong for you, darling," Justin said through his tears. But it's hard for me, too. It's so hard. Life is so cruel. This is another reason why I don't believe in God. Why would He do something like that? We didn't do anything wrong." I could tell how affected he was. Not only was it the first time he cried for our baby, but it was the first time I'd ever seen Justin cry at all.

"I know," I said. "The only thing I prayed for, every day during this pregnancy, was to have a healthy baby. You don't have to be strong for me. You're still human. I love you, and I'm so sorry, baby."

The next morning, I was up at four. I couldn't sleep. In tears, I called my twin sister in Paris to explain what was happening. With the time difference, I hadn't been able to reach her before.

Then it was time to go. We arrived at the hospital at 6:45 a.m. and finished the paperwork by ten. Every time a nurse came to talk to me, she asked for my identity and why I was there. It was unbearable. I had to say "termination" too many times. They would take this life away, because they weren't how they were supposed to be. I didn't manage to finish my baby correctly. The guilt overtook me again. I was sobbing the whole time. Justin was there, holding my hand the whole way, until it was time to go into the theatre. He followed the team as they rolled my bed into the anaesthetic room, but then he had to leave me.

It was so distressing to be alone, surrounded by the medical team moving around me, each and every one of them having a job to do. They were about to take my baby away from me. It was my first time in surgery under general anaesthesia, and I couldn't stop crying.

I was then transferred to the theatre, where the lights were blindingly bright. They moved me from my bed to the operating table, and I was terrified as they put a mask on my face and had me breathe into it. The anaesthetist injected something into my IV, and I quickly fell asleep, tears still wet on my face. The only thing I recall was having a weird and bright dream.

The next thing I knew, I woke up where I started, on the bed I got into when I'd arrived. I asked for Justin straight away. I wanted to see him. The nurse called for him, and he was by my side within minutes. It was 1:15p.m., and it was over. I felt tired and disoriented, sad and lost. I was bleeding a lot down there. I'd just lost my baby, and I didn't have anything left in me… in my belly. Just their memory and the pictures of the ultrasound. Before I left, a nurse came to talk to me, wanting to make sure I would be okay. I was desperate, but she said that time would make things better. I would never forget, but the pain would soften.

The next few weeks were painful and sad. I couldn't get more than a few days off work, and my boss wanted me back. I was grieving while trying to come back to my normal life. I had to tell the people who'd been aware I was pregnant what happened, and every single time it broke my heart just a little bit more.

We hadn't wanted to know the gender. It was somehow easier not knowing what he/she was. Angels don't have a gender, anyway. Justin never really understood why it took me so long to grieve my baby, as he recovered quite quickly. After a couple of weeks, he told me to move on. Men and women are so different when it comes to emotions and life or death. For him, it was, "You live and then you die," and as death is part of life, when it happens, you just need to move on. I found that level of pragmatism harsh and insensitive.

Justin would get upset when I had to share my feelings, so after a few weeks, I kept my pain to myself. Finally, a few months after the loss, the routine took over, and we stopped talking about it. Also, I decided it was time to go back to my home country, France. I needed to be with my family. I wanted to hold them all in my arms. Planning for this trip saved me. I was thinking of something else; something healthier that I could look forward to. I loved travelling and organising trips. It would be Justin's first time in Europe, too. He'd met my sister when she came over in April that year, and my parents after our wedding a couple of years previous. Now he was the one to come to my country, and I was happy for him to discover where I came from, my roots, and the place that made me who I was.

Three months later, in October, we went to Paris to see my twin sister for a week and visited the entire city. We enjoyed drinking beers at brasserie terraces, eating the delicious pastries, and walking everywhere. I showed him where I used to live and the places I used to go to when I lived there. Then we went to Nice, the city where I was born. It's a beautiful small town on the French Riviera between Cannes and Monaco. We spent five days with my parents, visiting the surrounding old villages along the sea and savouring the local culinary specialties. I was revived. It was so good to show him my hometown and share all the things that I loved with him. He loved it, too.

We also went to Italy, as I'd always wanted to see Pisa, Firenze, and Roma, which was where Justin's auntie lived. It was fantastic. I felt alive again. Justin and I were happy and loving each other like never before. The loss of our child had been painful and disturbing for both of us, and we each dealt with it in our own way. But in the end, we were still there, together. That romantic time in my country helped us get over it and brought us closer.

But I wanted to get pregnant again, quickly. Even if everyone around me was telling me to take my time, for me, there was no time to waste. I wanted to move forward, turn the page, and try again. I didn't want to sit on this tragedy for too long.

I fell pregnant again when we got back from our wonderful trip in Europe. I was due exactly a year and one day after we lost our first baby. It would be our rainbow baby. We never would have been able to experience the joy they brought us if we'd had the first one, and somehow it was the only thing that helped me get over the loss of our baby angel.

2

So now here I am, on my third pregnancy, and I'm trying to do as little as possible, except at work. I'm a brand manager for three kitchen appliances brands in Australia, which means being under a lot of pressure and having crazy deadlines.

Three months ago, I'd discovered a small lump in my left armpit. My general practitioner said that maybe it was a swollen gland because of a cold. Though it started out small, it's gotten so big and painful, that I have trouble closing my arm. I mean, who gets a swollen gland under their armpit due to a cold? When I try to make an appointment with my GP, they tell me their first opening is in two weeks, so I decide to go to the emergency room at St. George's Hospital.

After waiting an hour, I'm examined by a doctor who seems quite worried and asks me a few questions while touching my armpits.

"Did you lose weight, or have you been tired recently?" he asks in a serious tone.

"Really? I'm thirty weeks pregnant, and I look like a balloon, so of course, I'm tired." I do my best to smile at him. "I've got a sixteen-month-old baby at home who always wants to be held and starts tantrums. And obviously I put on weight, not the other way around."

Though I'm laughing, his expression is so anxious, that I start to worry. I tell him what my GP told me about it being due to a cold, and he says they'll have to do an ultrasound before they make any diagnosis.

I let him know I tried to get an ultrasound, but I couldn't wait the two weeks it would take to see my GP, which was why I was here. I also ask if it could be breast cancer. The doctor says he can't say what it is until they do a scan, so they will admit me to get the ultrasound done."

I tell my boss that I will work from my hospital bed and spend the day worrying. I don't really need more problems. My auntie passed away from breast cancer when I was seventeen, and I know how hard it was for my cousins. I don't want that for my kids.

By the end of the day, I have my ultrasound and get the results. Another doctor explains that I have three inflamed lymph nodes, and the biggest one is three-by-two centimetres. But to identify exactly what kind of infection it is, we need to do a biopsy. When I ask if they can do one immediately, they tell me that they require the consent of my obstetrician or GP, as the local anaesthesia could slow down the baby's heart.

I'm devastated. Of course I don't want to harm the baby, but I'm so desperate to know what this stupid golf-ball-sized lump is. I call my GP straight away for an appointment the next day. Unfortunately, he doesn't want to make the decision and tells me to talk with the obstetrician.

The next morning, I'm back to work, but I can't stop thinking of the worst-case scenario. My boss, who comes into my office to get some updates about our big brand launch event, sees my worried face and asks if everything is all right. I tell him what's going on and how worried I am waiting for a diagnosis, and he tells me I just have to "suck it up."

With this pregnancy I've already had thyroid issues, varicose veins, progesterone treatments, and thrush. I'm just hoping that after all this, the baby will be perfect.

I remember how hard my second pregnancy was. I had headaches, I was hot all the time, and above all…was crazy emotional. My due date was July 26, 2014, and I'd been working hard for a promotion that wasn't coming as quickly as my boss had promised. Because, really, who gives a promotion to a pregnant lady in this man's world? I was exhausted and driving Justin crazy with my anxiety. We told Justin's dad, Stephen, and his partner, Belinda, on Christmas Eve, and they were super excited and happy for us.

During the first trimester, I was anxious something would go wrong after my first terrible experience, while Justin was pretty much in denial about the whole pregnancy. He was waiting for the thirteen-week ultrasound to acknowledge the baby in order to avoid another painful moment. I couldn't deal with it and felt lonely. We argued a lot. Maybe we were both scared of becoming parents.

He wasn't helping enough with the chores at home. I knew his work was demanding physically, but I couldn't do everything by myself anymore, on top of my job. My main concern was that if he was like that now, how would we function with a baby? I couldn't do it all by myself.

I started to get less worried only at the end of January, thirteen weeks in, when the ultrasound technician told us everything was fine with the baby. He had a brain, two arms and legs, and a beating heart, and that made me feel a little better. But my placenta was a bit low, so I had to limit my efforts until the next scan, six weeks later.

In February, we finally told everyone. Things were definitely getting better, and Justin was helping me around the house since I'd slowed down. We were also looking at buying a house for our family, but the auctions in Sydney were always about a hundred to two hundred thousand dollars higher than the market price our bank was willing to give us. Justin worked most Saturdays, so I had to visit houses by myself. After a couple of months of searching, my heart wasn't in it anymore, so we tried to focus on the arrival of our baby.

I also had to start picking out a day care centre, because it was hard to get a position for a baby, and the demand was high.

I thought it was a boy, but again, we wanted to be surprised. I imagined how good life would be with our child, our little creation, the mix of both of us. They would have Justin's eyes and hair but my study skills.

My pregnancy was considered "at risk" due to my placenta being low and lacking fluid. Otherwise, everything was fine. Justin and I were happy and excited to start our own little family. But it was difficult not having my sister and my parents there. Though Skype and Viber were great, some proximity would definitely have been better. I could never ask software to babysit, either.

It was still ten weeks before the birth of our baby, but one night when we got home, I felt the need to pack a hospital bag. Justin laughed and said, "You don't have to prepare your bag right now. Don't worry. You have plenty of time. Go to bed."

I relented.

That same night, at four a.m., I rushed to the toilet, thinking I was peeing myself but then realised that my water had broken. I called my sister in Paris, because with the time difference, I knew she would be awake.

She told me to go to the hospital and asked if Justin was with me. I explained that he was sleeping and that I was only at thirty weeks.

"Wake up Justin and go!" she said.

I called for Justin in a shy voice, as I felt guilty and scared. But Justin heard me and joined me in the bathroom. I was shaking, still holding my phone to my ear.

"Did your water break?" Justin asked, surprised.

"Yes, I think so…or maybe not." I tried to convince myself it wasn't happening.

"No, your water broke. We need to go to the hospital right now," Justin said firmly.

"No, no. Maybe we should call the hospital first."

"We need to go right now," he said. No need to call."

"But I'm only at thirty weeks. It's too early," I repeated. "I have to pack my bag. I need to have a shower and change my pants. They're wet."

"Please, we've got no time for that. Let's go," Justin said.

"Okay. I'll take a plastic bag to protect the car seat." Even through my panic, I grabbed the bag and shakily let Justin lead me out of the room.

I told my sister I loved her and hung up just before Justin helped me run the two flights of stairs to our car. He impressed me with his calm. I was nearly jealous, but also a bit upset, because I felt irrational being scared by the situation. My baby was about to come ten weeks earlier than expected. I'd read that thirty-three weeks was the safe mark to have a premature baby. Those three weeks would have made such a big difference. I was scared for my baby's life. I'd had weird contractions two weeks before, but my GP had told me I didn't have to go to the hospital. I just needed to rest. *Note for later: never listen to your GP but to your own instincts.*

When we arrived at St. George's hospital, we found out they couldn't care for babies with less than thirty-two weeks of gestation. They had to find another hospital with a Neonatal Intensive Care Unit (NICU) that was able to care for very premature babies.

To make sure the baby's lungs would be open enough for the birth, I received an injection of steroids. I also swallowed a tablet to delay the labour. Apparently, a baby could survive up to three weeks after the rupture of the membrane, with minimal water. Justin stayed by my side until they found a place for us at the Royal Hospital for Women in Randwick, about half an hour away.

I was transferred at sunrise, placed in a shared room, and given more steroids every twenty-four hours, as well as additional tablets to delay the labour for the following three days. That Sunday, Justin missed his remote-control car bash he'd organised with his mates. I felt bad for him and guilty for not being able to bring a pregnancy to term so far. It was my second one, and I'd been feeling anxious all the way because of what happened during the first one.

On Wednesday, May 21, 2014, after three long days lying in bed, hoping to keep my baby inside me for as long as possible, I started feeling contractions at 3:30 a.m. They got shorter and more intense throughout the day, but after some back and forth to the delivery suite and lots of monitoring, I was back in my room. The pain was intense, but the nurses told me it could take days. I wouldn't last that long. I couldn't sleep or even rest. By 8:30 p.m., Justin had spent the entire day by my side, so I told him to go back home. But two hours later, I called the nurse and let her know the contractions were even closer. After a quick check and a doctor visit, they said it was unlikely I'd give birth that night. I was sure they were wrong, though.

Around midnight, the contractions were four to five minutes apart but strong and painful in my lower back and abdomen. The midwives did a quick check and decided to get ready for the birth. They brought the resuscitation cart and delivery pack but had to prepare everything in my room, because there were no delivery suites available. My poor roommate was forty weeks pregnant and massive. She probably freaked out when she heard me screaming my head off and breathing like an animal.

I asked them to call Justin, but he wasn't answering his phone, and they couldn't leave a message. I'd asked him so many times to set up his bloody voicemail. The only people with me were a wonderful midwife and some other nurses. I was about to go through one of the most important moment of my life…alone.

"Calm down and breathe," the nurse said. "If you feel like pushing, please try to keep it inside. We still don't have a delivery suite."

"What? Sorry," I said, panicked. "How do I hold it inside? Are you serious?"

After a few minutes, they managed to get a room, and as they pulled my bed towards the elevator, I felt it. "I need to push now," I said. It was an amazing natural sensation, like the baby had to come out and was pushing through me.

They asked me to keep it inside, and I tried my hardest. By this point they'd been able to reach Justin and promised he'd be there soon, but I couldn't hold it anymore. My body demanded that I push.

"That's okay," they said. "Go for it."

As I was about to push a second time, we arrived in the delivery suite. The doctors asked me if I minded some students observing the delivery, because such an early birth didn't come around often. When I accepted, I hadn't realised there would be seven of them. But I didn't care. I was in so much discomfort. I just wanted my man. My grip on my midwife's hand was so tight I could probably have broken her bones. They gave me some gas, but it wasn't doing anything for me, and I tried to push the mask off my face with my mouth.

Just as they transferred me to the bed, Justin finally arrived. It was such a relief to see him. The pain was excruciating. Every time I pushed, I felt the baby's head trying to come out of me, literally distorting me from the inside. I could feel everything. They told me that I had to push one last time, or otherwise the baby could be in danger. So using all the energy I had left, I pushed as if it was the last thing I had to do in the world.

Once the head was out, the rest of the body slid easily out of me. They placed my baby on my bare chest for a couple of seconds, bottom up, like a little frog. These few seconds felt like minutes. It was such an intense moment. I already had so much love for this little thing.

Justin was by my side, holding my hands and telling me with a big smile and tears in his eyes, "It's a boy," while showing me his genitals. I was just happy it was over and that he was here and alive. But I was so glad it was a boy, just like we wanted. He was so tiny, I could cover his little body between my small two hands. He was the most beautiful thing I'd ever seen.

They asked us if we had a name for him. I looked at Justin and said, "Jack?" It was the name he'd always talked about. He replied that we'd think about it, but for me, it was sorted.

They quickly took my baby away to help him breathe and prepare him for the incubator. He was born at 1:19 a.m., measured forty-one centimetres, and weighed in at 1.42 kilograms. I called my sister and my dad in France, and everyone was excited to welcome the first son in our family in at least four generations. My dad couldn't have been happier.

We waited another four hours before they finally called us back to see our son. Justin and I did finally agree on the name Jack, which was his step-grandfather's name. He was a war hero and Justin's role model, and I liked the idea of a strong name.

Jack seemed so small in this box, connected to a respiratory machine, but he was the most beautiful baby in the world to me. I passed my hand through one of the holes on the side of the incubator. The palm of his hand was the size of my thumbnail, and he looked so fragile. Justin was sad and overwhelmed with all the tubes, wires, and noisy machines around us, but I tried to comfort him. I'd been a premature baby myself, and even if Jack was early, it was thirty-four years later. Nowadays, they could do miracles.

Then Justin went home, and I was taken back to my room to try and get some sleep, even if I had to pump my milk every three hours!

The next morning, I couldn't wait to see my beautiful boy. I went down to the NICU every three hours to give him the precious little drops of the first milk, colostrum, which is so important for his health. It was my way of apologising. All I wanted was to feel his little body skin to skin, hearbeat to heartbeat, and then it happened. The nurse positioned him on my bare chest and covered him quickly with a warm blanket. What an amazing sensation it was to feel him against me. I couldn't help the tears of happiness and fulfilment. I felt like I was whole again.

Every emotion I'd held since his birth finally came out. My heart was growing and about to explode with so much unconditional love. From now on, he would be my blood, my guts, my everything. My reason to live, to fight. My baby boy, forever. It was like I'd witnessed a miracle, something coming from the gods; an angel, pure and beautiful.

Justin and I contemplated our beautiful son, discovering his traits, his thin face, and every detail of his little body. He would just have to get bigger and stronger, and we could all go home. I couldn't help feeling guilty for his early birth, but I was so happy he was fine. He was my son, and together we would conquer the world. Nothing else mattered. Jack was my new priority.

We had a daily routine of changing his nappy, cleaning him a little, and giving him my milk. Then, for one hour a day, I had the chance to hold him on my chest, skin to skin, or *kangaroo care*, so he didn't get cold. When my twin sister and I were born, they hadn't known how vital kangaroo care was, and they didn't put us together, either. But now they're aware that keeping identical twins in close proximity helps them recover faster.

All I could do to help Jack get stronger was provide my care and love, and cuddle him daily. Justin got to hold him the second day, and he was so happy. I could see tears forming in his eyes. He was a dad, and I could tell how much he loved his son already. He was so proud.

Jack could breathe normally without the machine after twenty-four hours, but he had jaundice and stayed under a UV lamp for nearly three days. It looked like he was getting a tan, with his eyes covered by his little mask. But I was glad when the jaundice was gone.

After five days, I had to go home without my son, and that was heart-breaking. I saw all these mums leaving the hospital with balloons and flowers, their baby in their arms. I was still expressing milk every three hours and was exhausted and sad, missing Jack badly.

I started a diary for him, where I wrote every day of his progress and what he liked to do: smiling at me, stretching, yawning, and sleeping. It helped me cope with the anxiety and sadness of having my son fight for his life away from me. The NICU crew gave me the idea, and I loved it.

They also helped me collect the little things to remember his journey: his umbilical cord, the little UV protection mask, some wires, and his name tag. Also, one of the nurses drew a lovely sign with Jack's name for his incubator. After nearly a week without clothes, I discovered my baby wearing his first outfit. The nurses had given him a red bodysuit with long sleeves and legs that had a little blue elephant embroidered on the chest. It was still way too big for him, but by wearing it, he looked more like a *normal* baby, and he was so handsome.

I was exhausted, but I had to go every day. I couldn't help it. I needed to see him, to touch him, to take care of him. I knew that being there for him was his best medicine.

After twelve days, we were able to transfer Jack to our local hospital, and even though St. George's wasn't as modern, it was only ten minutes away, and I could go back and forth from home while he was asleep. The transfer made him sick for a couple of days, though. Every time he suffered, I would break internally. I couldn't stand seeing him sick or weak, or even sad.

I felt guilty for having worked so hard without considering my health better. I was outraged that in Australia, there was no obligation for an employer to pay maternity leave. It puts so much worry and financial pressure on young couples, and it's physically demanding to work until the last minute. I'd never seen so many premature births around me. I came from a country where it was compulsory for women to go on maternity leave six to eight weeks before birth. My sister's best friend, who'd been pregnant at the same time and experienced the same pregnancy conditions, was put on bedrest, and her boy was born healthy at thirty-seven weeks.

I spent every day sitting next to Jack, feeding him by the tube, and then trying to breastfeed him. He wasn't strong enough to take the nipple properly, so we had to bottle feed him as well. He would take an entire hour to drink eighty millilitres of milk. The doctors were also worried, because his oxygen levels dropped, and he choked sometimes while feeding.

We weighed him every two days to make sure he was growing. Just gaining a few grams was a victory; growing a few millimetres was relieving. Justin would join me after he was done at work, and we took turns bathing him. The little time we got to touch Jack was unbelievably pleasurable. We looked forward to every little moment we could spend close to him.

After a month, I started to get desperate. I wanted him home with us. I couldn't stand the hospital anymore. It was too hard emotionally.

Justin and I were overtired. We'd get back home after nine p.m., eat quickly and poorly, and look at the empty crib in our bedroom.

On July 12, 2014, after fifty-two days in NICU, we finally left the hospital with our baby. We put Jack in his baby car seat, still too big for him, and drove him home. That day was one of the happiest of my life. I showed him around the flat and explained where his bed was and how things would go from there. Then I told him how glad we were to finally be reunited as a family.

He didn't sleep through the night until he was six months old. And even after that, he struggled. I expressed milk every three hours, and it took an hour to feed him on top of that. I felt exhausted constantly. Because I was producing so much milk. I was a month's supply ahead and had to buy a big new freezer. I felt like a cow during my short maternity leave and tried to wean off in November, so I could go back to work in December without having to express anymore.

Giving Jack my milk was my way to help him have a good start in life. The NICU nurses, as great as they were, kind of brainwashed me by telling me how important it was to breastfeed your baby. It became my obsession, and I felt like a bad mum if I wasn't pumping. I think that it's hard enough for parents with babies in the NICU, and that you shouldn't feel pressured to breastfeed, especially when it takes an hour. The rest and mental health of the mum should come first. Whether the milk comes from their breast or a formula, at the end of the day, mum needs to be at her best to cope with all the issues such a premature baby brings into her life.

My parents came to Australia for five weeks, from mid-August until the end of September. We all lived in the same small flat. It was nice to have them with us. During that time, I thought about how hard it must be for them to live so far away from me and their grandson. Now that I was a mum, I got it. I also thought about how hard it was going to be for us. There'd be nobody to take care of Jack if we required some time off, and he was growing so fast.

He started day care two days a week in November. He was the youngest at the place, and the staff was unprepared for him. I understood that in Australia, many mums stayed at home with their baby for an entire year, so that might have explained why most centres weren't used to young babies. In France, all mums go back to work and leave their baby at day care after four months of maternity leave. Another difference I learned was how insanely costly it was here.

But as Jack and I got closer, Justin and I were drifting apart. He spent most of his time on his smartphone, connecting with the remote-control car Facebook group he'd created. No matter what I said, he felt attacked. I would be back to work soon, and he still expected me to take care of the household and the baby on top of it. I hoped things would get better once I went back to work. When I have too much free time, I start arguing a lot, probably due to intellectual boredom or lack of self-esteem.

Going back fulltime was difficult after such a short maternity leave. Every morning I would tell Jack how I'd miss him, but that I had to make a living. Then I'd cry in my car. I wasn't happy in my job anymore and was resentful for this early birth. But I tried to spend all my free time playing with him, nursing him, and enjoying his smiles and laughter.

And things did get better with Justin. He helped out with a few things at home, and even if it wasn't much, I could have a quiet shower, the dream of every mum. He'd also wake up on weekends to let me sleep in. I was working hard again, but this time it was more so I could finish on time and come home to my son.

I had to launch a new brand. My boss hadn't done anything during my maternity leave, because he'd been waiting until the last minute again to request miracles from me. Though I'd lost my old assistant and the product manager, I did have a new assistant, who was a motivated undergraduate, full of energy and a perfectionist like I was. I thought about looking for another job, but I wanted another baby quickly, and I figured it was better than diving into the unknown, especially when I had to adjust to motherhood. Plus, the people were nice.

In February, Jack started to crawl and roll. Within five minutes, he could be on the other side of the room. He still had his blue eyes and dark blond hair and looked a lot like me. He was adorable, cheeky, affectionate, and so funny. He was curious about his surroundings, and his behaviour surprised me every day. He began waking up at night again, and between the sleeplessness and my job, I was exhausted. I started to think maybe I was pregnant again. Justin and I wanted a second baby, and we never used contraception anymore.

Even if I had to sacrifice my favourite hobby, sleeping, Jack was such a joy. Always happy and so innocent. Just his smile made me feel good every day. My sister got pregnant again on Jack's birthday. The twins, Liam and Lana, were born at seven months, in December, and were happy and healthy. She'd had always wanted a boy and a girl. I thought many times about how it would have been nice to live in the same city, or at least the same country, so the cousins could grow up together.

She was glad to be able to understand that as twins, her children had such a special relationship. They'd also stayed about fifty days at the hospital. The same journey, the same pain, the same long wait, the same issues. Only for her it was twice as hard, with a three-year-old daughter on top of it all. I felt bad I couldn't be there for her. I'd given my parents Jack's premature clothes, and I was glad to see pictures of my nephew and niece with my son's little outfits. They were in the same incubator and crib and were always holding hands and looking at each other. It was sort of painful for my twin and me. Though we were happy to see them so close, we couldn't help thinking how we would have loved that for ourselves.

I also made it my mission to lose the maternity weight by going back to the gym and doing a quick detox diet, which I convinced Justin to do as well.

Jack had begun standing already, and he could walk with us if we held his hands. At seven months, he was early. Within three weeks, he went from crawling and rolling to walking. He loved going to the park, laughing in the swing, and going down the slide. He also loved watching the waves at the beach and playing with us at home. Though he was going through a separation anxiety period, I tried my best to cuddle him as much as I could, so he could sleep better at night.

On March twelfth, I handed Justin a little silk sachet, like the ones that hold jewellery.

When he opened it, he pulled out a dried little chickpea and tried to bite it.

"Don't do that. You wouldn't want to eat your second baby, would you?" I asked with a grin, struggling to form my words due to my excitement.

"That's it? Already?" He was really surprised and almost worried. We were always exhausted, because Jack wasn't sleeping through. and he'd been helping me at night.

"Yes. Isn't it awesome? I know it's hard at the moment with Jack, but I'm hoping it won't last. We always wanted our two kids to be close in age, so that's great. Anyway, it's better to do all the nappy and baby stuff now. We'll suffer for the next three years, and then it will be over, once for all. I'm so excited," I said, babbling. "I'd like a girl this time. I mean, as long as it's healthy, it's okay, but I've always wanted a boy and a girl, so it would be perfect." I gave him a kiss and curled myself into his arms.

"Me too," he said. "It will be a girl, anyway, and she will be awesome and super nice to her daddy, and she will let him sleep." He laughed.

I'd even given Jack my favourite doll so he could practice for his little sister, and though he was torturing it, he still had nine months to learn.

That day, Jack walked by himself for the first time, pushing the musical lion walker along. I couldn't hold back my tears of joy and pride. He wasn't even ten months old, and he was looking for his independence already.

During my first trimester, Jack was sick a lot, sleeping in our bed most of the time and always wanting me to hold him. Five weeks into my pregnancy, I found out I had hypothyroidism, which meant that my thyroid wasn't working as much as it should, and it could be damaging to the baby. I hoped we didn't find out too late and started a treatment straight away. No wonder I'd been so tired. That certainly couldn't have helped.

Jack had a good bedtime routine, but he still wasn't sleeping through the night. We brought him to Tresillian, a hospital facility for babies, where we could learn controlled crying techniques. I developed the ability to differentiate between the distressed cries and the tantrum ones. Eventually Jack slept through but would wake up at around 4:30 or five in the morning. At least he stayed in his bed, which brought back peace and harmony between Justin and me.

In May, we celebrated Jack's first birthday. He stood without help and played all day with the balloons we'd decorated the garden with. We brought him to swimming lessons every Saturday morning, and he loved it. Especially babbling with the other babies. My first trimester went quickly, and I was already eighteen weeks pregnant. I had a feeling it would be a girl. I couldn't help myself. I had to eat chocolate and sweets on a daily basis. I tried to resist, but it was stronger than I was. Both my sisters craved chocolate when they were pregnant with their girls. I was hoping it was a sign, even if it meant I had to gain a fair bit of weight in my butt.

At that point, everyone at work knew that I was pregnant again, and my boss was getting more annoying. I worked hard, and yet I felt like I had to prove myself even more. I'd done so much in so little time, with the help of only one assistant. I promised myself that after this pregnancy, he would never see me again.

I had to go to an out-of-town conference for three days. The only good thing to come out of it was the nice body massage I had on the activity day. Finally, I had a day for myself, when I could rest a bit and take a breather.

I was happy to come home to my boys and nicely surprised that Justin had coped for three entire days, taking care of our son by himself. Jack cried a lot after me, but overall it went well, and this time off reassured me of my husband's capacity to hold down the fort without super mummy.

My body was going through hell. My thyroid was now stable, but I got varicose veins in my groin and on the top of my right leg. I could barely walk. The doctors told me to avoid moving too much and rest as much as I could. Right. Between my job and my one-year-old son who wanted to be held all the time, not to mention the four flights of stairs at home, this wasn't possible.

Also, the obstetrician told me that maybe Jack was born early because I terminated another pregnancy not long before falling pregnant again, so they started giving me a progesterone treatment. I couldn't believe my ears. If chances were higher after the termination, why hadn't they done something for my second pregnancy or at least been put on bed rest? I prayed every night to have a healthy baby, born to term this time.

Jack hadn't gained any weight in the last six months. Despite asking the paediatrician to solve the problem, she waited a long time to let me know that stopping his reflux medicine was certainly the issue. And sure enough, when Jack started his treatment again, he began regaining some weight. I was upset but relieved we were finally doing something about it.

Jack walked around everywhere now and had received his first haircut. He looked like a little boy and had eight teeth already. He could clap his hands, wave goodbye, clack his tongue, throw the ball, take off his shoes, and spoon-feed himself. He loved to draw, paint, stack up Legos, and talk to us. Even if we didn't understand, it seemed like real serious conversations.

He needed surgery to remove the hydrocele (swelling) he'd had in his testis since his birth in November. It was nothing too serious, but it could have become a hernia, so we had to do it soon.

Since he'd gone back on his reflux medicine, he was waking up at night again, and it was exhausting for us. But even with his constant health issues, Jack was such a blessing. He was a wonderful and special little boy, and I loved him more every day. But he was taking up so much space in our couple life, that it was hard for Justin and me to adjust. I was always looking for ways to positively re-energise ourselves as a couple. We tried to have a ten-minute chat every night or every second day. But Justin was tired, too. He was getting shorter and shorter with me, swearing, and smoking cigarettes down in the garage for hours at night. I missed my gentleman, so I figured it would be nice for all of us to go to France in April, before Jack turned two.

I was already organising a week away in Normandy with my sister and her kids, so we could all be together in a big house close to the beach. I missed my family. Even though they were far from perfect, I loved them, and I wanted to be with them. It had become harder since we had babies, and I couldn't help thinking that it would be so nice to live closer to my sister and my nephews, as well as my parents. Home was anywhere, as long as I was with my family.

Finally, Jack had his surgery for his hydrocele during the last week of August. I was so scared, waiting for him to be released. He should have been out earlier. I could only wonder if my baby was okay. I started looking at the clock on the wall. It was so long waiting for my sweet boy. I held onto my unborn baby, touching my belly to comfort me, when they finally called me. But that night, Jack developed a high fever and was shaking badly. I'd never seen him like that. I was scared and drove him to emergency. They thought maybe it was a bad reaction due to a cold.

After thirty hours under an oxygen mask, my poor baby was pitiful and looked miserable, but he was so brave and wanted to play.

And yet, through it all, I was happy to be pregnant and having babies so close to one another, knowing they would be friends and accomplices.

3

It's October 8, 2015, and I'm finally having my biopsy. It took me a full month, because I had to wait two weeks to see the obstetrician, who said it was perfectly fine to do a biopsy even though I was pregnant, but still requested a referral from my GP. So I had to go to my GP again to receive the referral. It's painful, but nothing compared to my fear. I look at the big needle entering this now massive lump and get my tissues out. Two biopsies later, I'm done. Then I'm told the surgeon wants to see me next Thursday, maybe earlier, if needed. I have no idea what that means, and I don't want to.

I spend the weekend filled with anxiety. I'll have to go to work on Monday, hoping that everything's going to be all right. And it is…until I receive a phone call at around ten a.m. from the surgeon's receptionist. She says he wants to see me this afternoon at three p.m. I'm in shock. What does it mean? Does he have bad news? I call Justin and ask him to be at the appointment with me. I'm afraid something is wrong, and I don't have the strength to go by myself. I'm scared to death.

While waiting to leave the office for my appointment, I talk to my workmate, Stéphanie. My thoughts are driving me mad, and I need to vent to someone. She's scared for me, but we both hope it's going to be fine and that if we do cry, they will be tears of relief. I advise my boss that I have to finish early and leave the office after lunch. Then I pick up Justin at home, and we walk together to the breast and thyroid surgeon's private suite at St. George's Hospital.

The wait to see the surgeon feels like forever. I'm touching my belly, praying it's going to be fine, while holding onto my baby to compose myself. Justin tries to make me laugh to divert me from thinking about what happens next.

The doctor finally calls us in, and while closing the door behind us, he says, "So we've got the results of your biopsies."

"And? It's bad… Isn't it?" I ask.

"I'm afraid so. You have melanoma."

"Melanoma?" I'm a bit confused, as I'm not sure if it's cancer. I look at Justin, who's holding my hand tightly.

"Yes, it's a very aggressive skin cancer, and you're unfortunately at stage three, at least. Apparently, there's no primary cause. I'm sorry."

I again turn to Justin, my lips clamped tightly together in speechless terror. I feel tears slowly coming up, but I don't let them out. I want to stay as focused as possible and make sure I understand everything. I just gasp and try to swallow the ball forming in my throat. I'm wiping the stray tears away as Justin tightens his grip on my hands.

"Is the baby okay?" I ask, worried.

"Yes. Usually the placenta protects the baby, but you'll have to deliver it as soon as possible, so we can determine your stage and start treatment. I'm going to refer you to an excellent surgeon who specialises in melanoma at the Melanoma Institute Australia."

"But we wanted this baby to go full term" I say. "My son was already premature." Again, when I look at Justin, I could tell he's now in frozen mode.

"I understand, but melanoma is quite aggressive, and you need to get treatment as soon as possible. So next time you see your obstetrician, you'll have to tell her and start organising the birth. Do you have any questions?"

"No," I say, just wanting to get out of here, fast.

The doctor hands me the surgeon's business card and tells me his receptionist will organise an appointment for next week. "Meanwhile," he says, "don't hesitate to contact me if you have any questions."

We leave the office, and as I stop to pay the receptionist, she lets me know the details of my appointment with the other surgeon. Justin and I exit the private suite in silence, shocked, like someone just died in front of us. But it's me. I'm dying. A new life is growing inside me, and I may not be there for them. After a few steps into the hospital corridor, we stop and fall into each other's arms to cry like we never have before. The world around us is falling apart, and we're devastated. We hold onto these tears for what seems an eternity, after trying to stay composed in front of the specialist. But now we're exorcising the fear and shock out of our systems, freeing all the tension. When we're done, we're out of breath, not able to move anymore. The weight of the news is so heavy, the consequences so big. I can die in the next few weeks. My life is at stake, and so is my family. All I ever wanted is right in front of me, and now it may be taken away. It's so surreal and confusing.

I ask my husband, "Melanoma is cancer, right?" He just nods. And we cry again so hard, holding each other, leaning onto each other to avoid falling. Devastated. Powerless. An excruciating pain in my gut is trying to come out of my mouth, but I choke, and I'm overflowing with tears, unable to control myself anymore. I let everything out, expelling all the fear, the pain, the extreme sadness, and realise that what I thought impossible just became possible. It's happening to me.

So this is how it feels to be told, "You have cancer." I would never have imagined that. Your entire world is shaken. Everything around you seems so superficial. You don't look sick, but you're dying, and nobody can see it. And you don't know when it's going to happen. It's like you have a deadline. You feel under pressure, and a lot of questions go through your mind. I feel terrible for my family. I don't want to let them down. Two babies are hard to handle. I need to stay and help Justin, otherwise it's going to be so hard on him. Now that I have so much to live for, I hope I will have time to enjoy it all.

When we arrive home, I ask Justin for one night of crying; one night of feeling sorry for myself, before trying to have positive thoughts tomorrow, because he doesn't believe that feeling sorry for yourself helps anyone. When I came home without Jack the first night, he didn't let me cry for long. But tonight, I need it. I ask him to understand, and somehow, I think he needs it, too. So we cry together after putting Jack to bed, because we don't want him to worry or wonder what's wrong with Mummy and Daddy. I empty myself of the pain and sorrows.

I'm overwhelmed by the worst-case scenarios and bring myself so far down that I can understand how dying could bring me relief. And when I reach the darkest edges of my mind, I can feel the light within me, signifying all the things I'm not ready to lose, shining brightly. I think about all that I've achieved since I was born and the obstacles I've encountered within a life now shortened. Surviving all of that, and getting stronger because of it, has prepared me for this very moment. So I could now be strong enough. I won't die without a fierce fight. Justin, my kids, my sister, and parents…they need me. I can't let them down. Not now.

I'm scared and feeling guilty for possibly having to abandon my family. I don't want that. I can't believe it's happening to me, especially with my relatives so far away. I came to Australia, so my children could have a better future. I don't want them to live without their mum, and I want to be there for them and their own children. Justin has enough trouble taking care of one baby for a few hours, much less two for a lifetime. No way would I do that to him. He needs me; they need me. I have to defeat this beast.

It's crucial for me to not only survive but to get healthy. I remember how traumatic it was for me when my mum became ill, and my dad struggled to take care of us.

During childhood, my life was all pink and happy. I guess children have a great ability to look at the positive side of things. I was lucky to always have food on the table, and though my parents thought designer brands were a waste of money, I had clean and proper clothes to wear.

I was a good student and loved school. All of my spare time was spent with my twin sister, Laetitia, and we were inseparable. We didn't bother talking to the rest of the world until we were over two years old, probably because life together was pretty good, and we didn't need anybody else. My twin has been my other half since our conception, and even with the distance between us, we've stayed close and couldn't live without one another. She was always my best friend and confidante, so I never developed much of a social life. I lived for my marks and making my parents proud of me.

Laetitia and I are quite different She was always more creative, and I was more analytical. I performed well at school, while she didn't seem really interested. We were competitive, and being compared to each other all the time didn't help. My parents decided to place us in separate classrooms after two years at school, because the competition had a negative impact on us. Still, we were the best accomplices at all times. School was for learning, and home was for family.

I've always been a driven person, so I spent the first thirteen years of my life learning and trying to always be the best in class. Even the small things in life were about getting some learning out of it. I also enjoyed holidays and spent all my summers in a holiday camp managed by the company my dad worked for as an engineer. Since I was four years old, every July I'd go with my sister somewhere in France, by bus, hours away from home. It was hard at the beginning, being without Mum and Dad, but I had my sister, and we loved spending time riding bikes or ponies, climbing, or just playing games with the other kids, sons and daughters of Dad's workmates. There were the same families, year after year. Growing up, I looked forward to this time of adventure and independence.

I stopped going there when I was fourteen. I was in secondary school then and felt like I was getting too old for it. My parents thought it would be good for my sister and me to improve our English skills by going to London and living with an English family for a month. So we went there in July 1995 and stayed with a nice couple and their dog, going to English classes in the morning and spending our afternoons visiting the big city.

We loved it so much that we did it again the year after, this time with two separate families and without lessons. We visited every inch of the capital, immersed in the English culture for two weeks. It was such an adventure and quite a change. Different country, different money, different language, different architecture, different shops, and different way of life.

We spent the third and final week apart, as I had to follow my family on a weird holiday in Clacton-On-Sea. We lived in the caravan they owned in the local caravan park. Their twelve-year-old daughter gambled while her mum played bingo all day, every day. I didn't understand how she could waste all the money she'd been saving all year long. But these two episodes of a London getaway gave me a taste for adventure and exploring new horizons.

We were a close family. We'd spend winter holidays skiing together and usually the first two weeks of August in the Alps, hiking together.

Mum was the affectionate one, and Dad was the teacher. Julie, my big sister, was kind of a loner, and Laetitia and I were the inseparable pair. But we all had great times. And even if the daily routine was often full of arguments, we had lots of love for each other.

Since the age of five, I'd wanted to find The One, get married, and become a mum. I had my first crush at summer camp. His name was Thibault. He was a confident boy with dark hair and a pretty face, always ready to lead the other boys into some kind of game. But I didn't know that you had to ask someone to go out on a date with you. I didn't even know what going out meant. I missed the boat with him. A popular girl asked him out first, and he accepted. I was shocked when he told me that he would have accepted if I'd asked first, but I'd thought these things happened naturally, like in the movies. Anyway, I learned my lesson, and it was my first step to understanding men. But it still took me two more years to actually date someone.

It was 1995, and I was at the end of secondary school. I was raised with no real knowledge of fashion and was a sort of a tomboy up until then, dressing up casually, with no real effort. I didn't wear any makeup, either, but back then, not many girls did at fourteen, anyway. I wore glasses (the not-so-pretty ones), I was first in my class (not so cool at the time), I had a twin sister (it was hard when you constantly get compared), and my mum worked in my school. We also lived in the flat above the school building, as it was part of her salary package. Let's just say, I didn't have it easy with my schoolmates.

I wasn't popular. I couldn't even understand what the point of popularity was, so I focused on my studies. I didn't know what I wanted to become and could only see two weeks into my future. However, I decided to change my look, because I realised that my appearance mattered if I wanted to get some positive attention. I begged my mum to get me contacts instead of glasses, and she gave up after a month of resistance and a devastating letter explaining how I would feel so much better in my skin without them.

After a few makeover lessons from my best friend, Mélanie, I got a bit more confidence. Louis, a tall bloke with dark hair and brown eyes, was already in my classroom, but we started dating the following year. He was all my firsts: first kiss, first date, first pubs, first clubbing, first intimacy, but really first love.

When I look back on it now, I realise I couldn't have been that bad, because at least eight boys asked me out before Louis did. But I respected my mum's rule about no dating, because I was too young. When Louis did ask me out, there was no way I was going to answer with, "Sorry, Mum doesn't want me to." I didn't want to lie, and I still can't believe I was actually giving this answer when the boys I liked asked me out. You can imagine their faces and their laughter when they heard my excuse. For Louis, I justified my rebellion and didn't tell my mum until two weeks later, when she was cooking us some beef patties for lunch.

I said, "You know how you told me I couldn't date anyone, because I'm too young? Well, I'm fourteen now, and some of my friends have been dating since they were like twelve years old. I mean, if someone asks me out now, can I say yes if I want to?" I was pretending that it hadn't happened yet, and I was just checking on the status of this rule.

"Are you dating someone?" she asked and smiled with surprise.

"Maybe. And if I was, would you be mad at me?" I asked, hesitant.

In an amused tone, she said, "You're still young. That won't last, anyway."

"Yeah, right," I said, trying to sound neutral. "But it's not because I'm young that it won't last. I don't think my age has anything to do with it."

Somehow, she gave me the green light, but I was upset she didn't realise how important it was for me. After only a couple of weeks dating Louis, I was very much into him already. It was mutual, and I was so happy he'd asked me out. Later that day, he called on the home phone, and even though I rushed to get it, my mum would take the call first. We didn't have any mobile phones then, and there was no such a thing as privacy for us teenagers.

She said, "It's for you. It's a boy." Her tone told me she was clearly excited for me, but there was still a question in her voice.

I had a quick chat with him about our plans for the afternoon and hung up.

"Who was he?" Mum asked.

"It was Louis. "Louis who? Is that your boyfriend?" she asked with way too much enthusiasm.

"Just Louis. And yes, he is. Now, stop questioning me." I felt embarrassed.

Mum was wrong, finally. It lasted. The more time we spent together, the more I thought we were meant to be, and we understood each other so well. We were happy and in love. After a first kiss sealed our relationship at a girlfriend's party, weeks, and then months went by. We went out to the movies, then cafés, fuss ball, and pool. After a couple of years, it was clubs, car trips, and weekends in the country. We were at the end of high school already and stayed side by side all those years, even becoming popular without asking for it. We were the record-breaking couple in terms of our long-lasting relationship, and the other teenagers were inspired but envious somehow.

We used to love talking about anything and everything. We'd discuss life and the world society and relationships, and our plans for the future. He was a sort of revenge on the insecure child I used to be. With him, I was becoming a woman. Though still focused on my studies, I was also socially respected. At last, I had a proper social life. But my most important lesson was that I could finally understand men. I felt lucky to have found love so young, because the nearly four years I spent with him shaped the woman I became. I got to figure out what was going on in his head as I witnessed the transformation of a boy into a man.

Louis was my age. He was sporty and passionate about squash. He was a below-average student but a funny guy and an opinion leader. He had two brothers who were fourteen and ten years older than he was, which gave him some advantages when it came to intimacy. We were loyal and crazy in love. Yet, my twin was part of our lives, and he was aware of how important she was to me, especially since we'd known each other since we were seven years old. After so many years of social difficulties, I was finally happy. And my grades were fantastic, too.

But then, on June 6, 1997, my pink life changed to black.

I woke up early that morning to go to my high school math class. It was an exam day. As always, I was prepared but decided to check my notes before leaving home. When I went to the toilet, I was shocked by the sight of my mum lying on the floor.

"Mum? What are you doing?" She didn't answer, yet her eyes were open, and I could tell she understood what I was saying. "Mum? Are you okay? Let me help you." I tried to lift her up, but she was as heavy as a dead body. It was too hard, and I needed help. "Don't worry, I'll get Dad. Stay awake."

I went to my parents' bedroom. We weren't allowed to wake up my dad on the days he slept in, but I didn't hesitate to rush to his bedside.

"Dad, I'm sorry to wake you up, but I really need your help. Mum is on the floor."

"What?" My dad asked, rousing from sleep.

"Mum is lying on the floor. I've tried to get her up, but she's super heavy. I can't do it by myself. You need to come."

"Is she conscious?" he asked while following me.

"Her eyes are open. She's conscious, but she doesn't answer…" I explained as we reached the bathroom.

We got her up and placed her on her side of the bed.

"Do you want some water?" he asked her, but she didn't answer.

"We need to call the firemen, Dad." In France, they're the best ones to call in case of a medical emergency.

"No, that's okay. Go to school, I'll take care of her," my dad said firmly.

"But Dad, are you sure? I can stay. I'm worried for Mum."

"That's fine. Get ready and go. You'll be back soon, anyway." He was right. I only had class for three hours, and I would be back for lunch.

"Please call the firemen, Dad," I begged him before I left.

"I will call SOS doctors," he said to reassure me. They were a sort of emergency GP.

I was worried, because my dad didn't seem too anxious and wasn't quick to call a doctor. He didn't like them. The further away he could be from them, the better. I wasn't like that. Looking at my mum, I knew something wasn't right, and we had to do something fast. But I listened to my dad and left for school.

I felt overwhelmed, not knowing what Dad was doing. Louis was waiting for me downstairs with my daily breakfast, some Nutella pancakes his mum had cooked for us. I wasn't hungry. I told him what I'd just witnessed, and he tried to comfort me while we walked to school.

After a bad diagnosis from the SOS doctors, two hours later, my dad called our GP, who rushed them to the Emergency Room of our local hospital. She was the victim of a stroke. Sometimes, I wonder if I shouldn't have stayed that day and if I did well listening to my dad.

This tragic episode forever changed all of us as individuals and as a family. At sixteen, I transferred from childhood to adulthood in only a couple of months. I had no choice. With Mum spending nearly a year in hospitals, not being able to talk, the right side of her body disabled, my family balance was shattered. Mum wasn't there anymore to hold us together, and there wasn't such a thing as family after that.

At this point in my life, my dad was merely a banker for the misunderstood teenager I was. His only interaction with me was to give me pocket money every month, and he never really talked to me except to ask about my grades or help with my homework. He would visit Mum after work and never used to come home before 9:30 p.m. anymore.

Laetitia and I both felt like our big sister Julie was trying to replace Mum, which got us into so many arguments. Julie was eighteen already and spent her time studying in a nearby city, seeing her boyfriend, Olivier, at night, or helping me with the home chores before leaving again on the weekends to be with him. I felt trapped in the house and alone. I didn't see my mum or my dad very much anymore. My big sister was always with her boyfriend, while Laetitia was too sad to accept what was happening and preferred going out with her mates and the Swiss Italian boyfriend she was seeing at the time. Nothing was the same anymore. I was discovering the dark side of reality.

Louis and I no longer spent much time together, as it was hard to get away from chores and homework. And even if I did go out with my friends, I felt lonely, misunderstood, and guilty. I even wondered if it wouldn't have been easier if Mum had died that day. Life became so painful after her hospitalisation. Louis didn't understand how hard it was for me, and he didn't help the tragedy of the situation by breaking up with me a few months before our high school exams.

After nearly four years together, in April 1999, he drove me to our favourite beach and told me that it was over. He cried so much that I nearly felt sorry for him and didn't quite get why he was breaking up with me if it made him so sad. As an added nice touch, I was no longer able to go there anymore without thinking about this incident. *Take note: never break up in a place you love to visit.*

Mum was still living at the hospital then, and I was overwhelmed by sadness, studies, and chores. Every night, I cried like crazy in the shower, so no one could hear me. I felt stupid and hopeless. It was even worse once I realised Louis was a cheater. I didn't know it at first, but six months after our breakup, a common friend told me he'd slept with another girl at his place, after planning the thing for weeks. Meanwhile, I'd been studying and didn't see anything coming. He wasn't even brave enough to tell me the truth. After this episode, I definitely had trust issues with pretty much all my boyfriends. Still, he was the only guy I dated who knew my mum before and after her stroke.

I missed my mum. I wished I could talk to her, but every time I visited her at the hospital, I couldn't really communicate with her. I would tell her about school, but I never got any answers, because she couldn't talk anymore. One day, I saw her about to eat one of her anti-wrinkle creams, and I figured out she was in bad shape. She wasn't the same anymore. She was no longer the positive, tough, active, and strong woman I used to know. She seemed weak, distressed, and sad.

I confronted her, not wanting to accept the sad reality anymore. I begged her to make an effort and stop feeling sorry for herself all the time. She had to fight for us. We tried to give her paper and pen, so she could write some answers with her left hand, but it was difficult for her, especially since she was right-handed. With time, she started to talk again, like a kid would, with the brain finding other ways of reconnecting the synapses. Those eight months without my mum were distressing, and I had to confront my dad for the first time in my life.

Since I was born, Dad had always been the *Sunday Guy*. We never really did anything together except for Sundays and holidays. While we were growing up, he wouldn't accept me having a boyfriend, always thinking I was too young. With Dad, it was all about school, grades, work, and learning, because everything must be educational. I had another nickname for him: *No-fun Dad*. I constantly tried to be the boy he'd wanted, spending years of my childhood perfecting my rock-climbing and soccer skills. I wanted him to be proud of me, so I worked hard to get good marks at school, but he never told me that he was, until I passed business school. I had to ask him, and he said he'd always been proud of me, but the most important thing was for me to be proud of myself. *Note for dads: tell your kids you're proud of them. Don't wait twenty years.*

With Dad, I felt the answer would always be "no," regardless of what I asked. But it came time for me to tell him how I felt, even as I wondered if he'd be sensitive enough to get it. I decided to confront him one night as he was doing his daily crossword puzzle in the newspaper.

I approached him cautiously. "Dad?"

"Yes?" he answered, undisturbed, head down in the paper.

"We need talk about what's happening." I took a seat in the chair next to him.

"What's going on?" he asked, and I was glad to see him move the paper away.

"I'm not sure you're going to like what I'm about to say, but it's important to me. I really need you to understand, because we can't continue like this. It's not sustainable for me." I was trying to keep my calm and talk like the sixteen-year-old adult I was.

"Well, tell me, and we'll see then," he said, almost like a challenge.

"You know," I said, "I understand that the situation is hard for you, too, with Mum being your wife. It must be awful going through this. You nearly lost her, and now she's so different. But as painful as it is for you, it's hard for me and my sisters, too. It's our mum. She's always been there for us to talk to, and now we don't have anyone. I mean, we're teenagers. I wouldn't bother you about girl things. I can manage that by myself. But you need to be a dad."

"I am your dad. I'm here." I knew he was acting like he didn't understand what I meant.

"I'm sorry, but you're not really here. We cook, we clean, we do everything in the house to help you, and when you come home, you barely talk and don't even thank us for dinner. And most of the time we're already in bed. I mean, I'm happy to help, but I want you to understand that this situation is painful for us, too. We didn't ask for any of it. We have to do things that most sixteen-year-olds don't, and I'm sad to see what's happening to our family. Nobody is ever here anymore, including you. And I'm the one trying to keep up the place and bring us back together. Look, I just want you to be my dad and not my banker, okay?" I was now in tears. These words required so much strength. Saying this to my dad was excruciating.

I could tell he was trying to swallow his tears. It was the real first conversation we'd ever had, and I'd been harsh on him. But I needed him more than ever, and if I wanted things to change between us, it had to be said.

"I understand," he said, "and I will try to do better. But you know, you can talk to me any time."

"Can you give me a hug?" I asked, sounding more like I was begging.

"Of course," he said.

And with that, we fell into each other's arms, crying like we were relieved to be free of all the stress and anxiety that had accumulated over the past few months. I can see now that this conversation actually changed everything. Over time, and as we had more open conversations, we learned to understand each other better. It helped us develop a healthy and close relationship as father and daughter.

Mum wanted to come back home instead of going to a specialised rehabilitation centre that would have helped her get better faster. She took early retirement. The flat that was given to her due to her position as an administrative officer of my secondary school, wasn't set up for someone with a disability. This meant we had to move back to the apartment my parents had bought a few years before, which forced our tenants to move out. She was back home after so many months away. I was happy to have her close to me but so upset to see that she'd been changed forever into another woman.

She was unable to pronounce a sentence, could barely walk, and forgot all rules of good behaviour when interacting with others. The brain connections were slow to repair, and she was like a toddler, learning to speak, walk, and count again, but also how to behave socially. At least she'd kept her memory.

I became the mum, trying to help her with everything. Now that I was old enough, we could have gone shopping together, like my girlfriends were doing with their mums. She could have helped me with my Spanish lessons, as she had a degree in it. But at this point she could barely speak French and remembered only a few Spanish words that she sometimes placed in the middle of French sentences. I was angry at her, because I had to teach her everything again, such as writing with her left hand, pronouncing words properly, and just walking. I corrected her, helped her recover the rules of calculations, and to recognise names and numbers. But what disturbed me the most was that she didn't seem to understand anything I said, and we had trouble communicating.

It took her a few years to manage to walk again, with the help of a stick, as well as speak in full sentences, but she never recovered her right arm. Despite some physical improvements, neither of us has been the same. It's been like we've swapped roles.

4

That night, after the surgeon appointment, I decide to tell my family I have cancer. It's delicate and difficult. I call my sister first. She's devastated, saddened, and horrified. She's also scared it can happen to her now, since we're twins. I also tell Mum and Dad, who weirdly take the news well and don't seem to worry at all. Denial, maybe? I'm not sure, but somehow, I'm sad they don't understand the gravity of the situation and how badly it's affecting me and my family. I hold on to my tears when I let them know, trying to stay strong and practical to protect them. Maybe that's why they're not freaking out…or maybe they're trying to protect me. I actually do wonder how I'm going to do this with them being so far away. I wish they could be here by my side and that I could hug my sister and cry in her arms.

When I came to Australia five years ago, leaving everyone behind, I wanted every aspect of my life to change, and it happened in less than a year. This country called to me for a long time, and I finally flew the twenty thousand kilometres that separated me from the land of opportunity. Something I can't explain attracted me. For more than seven years, I'd struggled to find a way to do it...or maybe just the courage. But every time I thought of leaving everything behind, I found a good reason not to. If it wasn't my family, my grandma or my job, I was staying for a boyfriend. Until one day I ran out of excuses. I didn't have any boyfriend, I didn't have the job I wanted, and I was close to thirty years old. It was my time to be selfish and live my dreams.

My sister had fallen in love with the country when she was just eighteen and dating her first love, a French-Australian named Yohan. Her enthusiasm was so contagious, that when I had the opportunity to study at La Trobe University in Bendigo, I jumped on it, thinking this could be my opening to go there. But the spots to study on the Aussie campus were limited, and the chances of getting in were slim. So due to the logistics and finances involved, I decided on e-learning instead, which would run parallel to my BBA courses at my business school in Montpellier. And I figured I could always get a job or internship there later on.

I enjoyed learning about this part of the world, including the economics, geopolitics, culture and business relations of the Asia-Pacific region. And because I finished my first year at the top of my class, it would have guaranteed me a spot to study at the university. Unfortunately, it was too late. My decision had already been made and was irreversible. But I've often wondered what would have happened if I'd taken the chance.

Laetitia used to talk so much about Australia, that I was glad she finally got to visit this beautiful country in 2009. Every time she sent me pictures or called me from there, I was desperate to be with her discovering the big continent, rather than suffering from panic attacks due to a competitive colleague.

When I broke things off with my first boyfriend and decided to take a couple of weeks off to recover from work pressures, I was fired upon my return. Somehow, it was the best thing that could have happened to me. I wasn't getting any younger, but this "normal" way of life that I was raised into, just like everything else, was catching me from every corner. I wanted to see the world. I knew my family only wanted what was best for me, but they didn't realise that the way they were trying to help was bringing me down. They all encouraged me to get another marketing job. My sister lived in Paris, and since it was the capital, I figured there would be more opportunities, so I went there every month to attend interviews. But after eight months of unemployment, I was still looking for a marketing job while struggling to pay my bills and the rent for my studio apartment.

I was geographically flexible and willing to accept a lower salary package. The problem was that companies didn't trust in the future anymore. It was the Global Financial Crisis. There weren't many head offices, and most of them already had their marketing team, composed of one or two people at most. I also looked into internships in either the U.S.A. or Australia, but that endeavour was also unsuccessful. After passing a Bachelor Honours of Business and Administration, and achieving so much to give myself the keys to success, I felt like I'd hit a brick wall. Also, I was still searching for The One, now definitely late for our date. Maybe he was overseas? If he couldn't find me, I would have to travel and find him myself.

Then in March 2010, I got a three-month contract selling advertising for a monthly magazine in German and English that distributed on the French Riviera and overseas. It wasn't my dream job, but it was better than nothing. Here I was, nearly thirty and fantasizing about a different life. At the office, everyone was living their normal day-to-day life, nothing interfering with their routine. It was all so comfortable and predictable. I found it depressing. I wanted to achieve great things, be adventurous, and feel useful. I didn't want to be like everybody else. I knew I had to start over.

People at work were German or English and spoke in their own language. I was the only French person. This triggered me to realise how thirsty I was for new cultures, a new way of life. I felt trapped in my small country, sinking in its own too-conventional and conservative ways. There was a desperation inside of me to explore new horizons. I wasn't the problem anymore; France was. I loved my country, its food, its culture, and its beautiful landscapes, but on an economic level, some work had to be done.

I didn't want to be stuck in a routine. The thought of waking up, going to work, coming home, eating, sleeping, and doing it all over again, one day after another until I died, made me sick. I had to do something about it right away.

After three months of selling advertising, my contract was over. I told my boss that I didn't want to pursue this job, because I had other projects in mind. My decision had been made. I would leave.

I felt like a marionette, following my family's plan for my own life. I'd been playing nicely along so far, always asking for their recognition, approval, and praise, but I still felt like I was never good enough. I was always there for everyone else, putting them first. And then I looked around and noticed they were all settling down and moving forward with their lives and their careers. They were getting married and having kids. But not me. I kept feeling like I was living someone else's life and that somewhere in an alternate universe, I was much happier. With time, the heavy weight of my situation started to become a burden, slowing me down day after day. I wanted to free myself from it.

I was miserable and felt like nothing held me to this dying planet anymore, so I might as well die, too. I needed something that made me feel alive. I had to make my biggest dreams come true, so I'd have no regrets. This inspired me to start a bucket list, and skydiving was the first dream to tick off for my twenty-ninth birthday.

My parents tried to make it happen, but unfortunately, my skydiving experience was postponed by three days, so I didn't get to do it for my birthday. But I still spent it with my mum and dad. Despite the stormy weather, we had a good day. I smiled and laughed with them. We were a family, and most of all, happy to be together and knowing each other so well. My mum and I exchanged smiles, while Dad showed us photos of their last holidays. His dad used to do the same thing, and we'd all fall asleep on his lounge. We loved each other, and we demonstrated it. Sometimes it was in awkward ways, but the love was there.

The night before I would finally get to jump, my friend Nils picked me up and brought me back to his place, where we talked about everything and anything. He started asking me about my future plans and refreshing my memory about my wanting to go to Australia. He'd been there for three months the year before and knew it was my dream for the past seven years. It was second in line on my bucket list.

When I told him I'd been looking for a job in Paris, he said, "Are you sure you want to go there? Same streets, same mentality. It won't provide you with a real change."

"My family wants me to get a marketing job, but everything in France reminds me of my past."

"Why don't you go to Australia, then?" he asked. "It's been your dream since, like, forever."

I told him how I'd been thinking about it a lot lately, and that even though my family was probably right and I should get a proper job, I needed some spontaneity and wanted to improve my English.

I also told him about my online chat with my friend, Thomas, who now lived in Melbourne, and how one of his friends was the president of the French Alliance there. Plus, I had my degree from La Trobe Bendigo.

"Go then, just go… What's stopping you?" he asked.

"You're right," I said. "With no job or boyfriend, I have nothing to lose."

He showed me his postcards of the faraway country, telling me stories and things he experienced there. Listening to him reminded me of how much I wanted to go somewhere else and have new experiences with people who knew nothing about me or my past. I was seduced by the idea that I could start over and be like a brand-new person once I arrived.

It was nearly midnight, and I had to wake up early for my jump, so I decided I'd make my decision as soon as I landed back on Earth.

The next day, my alarm rang at eight a.m, waking me up slowly with a Pink song. I smiled for the first time in a very long time. It was the third day of my thirtieth year on this planet, and everything was going to be different after what I was about to experience. I knew I'd be transformed. I promised myself that I'd be happy and live every day to the fullest, without worrying about what people thought about my decisions.

I took a rushed but relaxing shower and put on a pair of jeans and a printed T-shirt of Mickey. Hey, it was a fun day, after all. My parents were offering me the sky, its immensity and beauty, and the feeling of understanding how small I am in this great big universe.

My dad finished packing everything into the cooler, and we were ready to go. I was happy, but also scared the jump may be postponed again, even if the weather was supposed to be fine for it. We arrived at 10:30 a.m. to jump base in Le Luc. The wide plain was surrounded by mountains like an arena, offering the promise of a wonderful view once I was high in the sky. Onsite, the mood was relaxed, and parachutists laughed together while having a coffee at the local café. It was a beautiful, warm day, and I felt the adrenalin in the air. We looked for the man in charge of my skydiving to check what time I'd jump. A tall, slightly bald, man in his forties welcomed us.

"Hi guys, I'm Patrick," he said with a smile. "I'll be Karine's instructor today."

After the introductions, he told me I would probably be able to do the jump around noon. My mum seemed impatient, so we killed time with a drink at the café. I watched the people jumping. They looked like pinheads, so high that I had trouble following the plane, big as my pinkie nail. How brave was I going to be once I was up there? I would be in the sky, in the atmosphere, higher than the birds. It was exciting and terrifying. The longer I had to wait, the more excited I got. Finally, I would have a proper start in the thirtieth year of my life when tons of emotions would meld together deep within my soul.

But when noon came, they said the heat could affect the balance of the parachute, and it was too dangerous to jump. We had to wait until four p.m., so we decided to go for lunch. We walked to the nearby forest and set our picnic spot close to a small creek where wild tortoises liked to rest. I felt guilty making my parents wait for so long and fill up their entire day just for my own pleasure. I knew my mum was impatient, and I felt even worse. But my dad placed the picnic on a large blanket, and we sat there in peace in the middle of this lovely décor, savouring our delicious salads.

I took advantage of a quiet moment to tell them about my idea of going to Australia later that year.

"By the way, I wanted to talk to you about my projects for autumn."

"Yes?" Dad said.

"Well, I've put a lot of thought into it, and as I'm still waiting to hear about this internship in the U.S., and it doesn't seem to be going anywhere, I was thinking I could still go overseas instead of to Paris. Because, after all, the real goal was to improve my English skills and get some international experience to help with future employment. So, I thought I could go to Australia, like I've always wanted to," I said, trying to show how reasonable I was being.

"Yeah, I guess. Why not?" Dad replied in between bites of his salad.

"Really? You would be okay?" I couldn't help but get excited. I told him how it would be cheaper to go to Australia, since I'd have to pay three thousand Euros to the company that would be providing my internship, while I could just purchase a ticket and get a casual job once I got there, as I looked for one that matched my skills and degree. "And also, if the U.S. internship does come through, my English will have improved. You know how hard it's been for me lately, and that's why I wanted to take this year to realise my dreams."

"Yes," he said. "We know how important it is for you, and anyway, it would be certainly be better for your resume to go overseas."

My dad was smiling at me, and I was nicely surprised by his new enthusiasm. He must have seen how much I was suffering trying to do things their way for so long, while sacrificing what was most important to me.

At four p.m., the manager decided that it was safe to jump. This time it was my turn, and my legs started shaking. I was nervous, but I couldn't be happier.

A blond guy in his thirties approached me. He told me his name was Eric, and he'd be my instructor and teammate for the dive. I would be attached to him, and we'd jump together. His confidence was palpable.

"Great. Where do we start?" I asked. "Are you going to teach me how we do this? I'm so excited but a bit scared, too. I mean, that's a crazy fall, right?" I wanted some kind of reassurance.

He told me he'd explain everything once we got on the plane. When I expressed concern, he said he'd done five thousand jumps, and he knew what he was doing. All I needed to do was relax and enjoy. I found him cheeky. "Getting high" and hooking up with a cute dude sounded pretty fun to me."

Eric helped me put on a full harness, to which he would attach himself once we were in the plane. I also got a pair of glasses specially made for skydivers, which I would have to wear just before jumping, and kissed my parents before joining the others on the launch area. There, Eric tightened my harness, and I followed him onto the plane with all the excitement and anxiety I'd accumulated so far. This was it!

The plane took off, and it was my first time not being attached to a proper seat. It was a small plane, and I was right next to the sliding door, trying to relax by listening to the jokes the guys were making. I noticed that I was the only woman on board, except for one of the videographers. I was also the only newbie.

As we got farther away, I could glimpse the sea now, and the coast from Fréjus to Toulon. When I asked Eric at what altitude we were, he told me two thousand meters. This surprised me. I was already shaking, and we were only halfway there. When I asked if we were going to be attached to one another, Eric suggested we strap ourselves in. Then Patrick, our videographer, said, "I'll go first and place myself at the sliding door, so I can film you as you're jumping out of the plane."

Eric told me to put on my glasses, and when we reached three thousand metres, he said, "When we jump, you'll have to curve yourself, pelvis to the front, while your body will be outside the plane, okay?"

"Okay," I said, terrified now.

He opened the sliding door. As the wind swept through the passenger compartment, I got startled and let a quick scream out of my chest. I was still scared, but I stayed strong and focused. I was a fighter and a modern woman, not afraid of adrenalin. Eric gave me the signal once Patrick was outside, waiting for us. It was my turn. I stood, shaking, with my body curved into space. Then I looked down… and saw it all. The height, the void, the four thousand metres between me and the ground. I was in the atmosphere of planet Earth, and I couldn't believe I was doing this. It was crazy. I really had trouble breathing now and tried to catch my breath like women do in the movies when they're having a baby. I was delivering me today. It was pure awesomeness.

Eric didn't warn me before propelling us out into this giant space. *Wow*, what a fall. At this moment, I wasn't thinking about anything anymore. I was screaming so hard with my mouth wide open. I'd never screamed like that. It came out of my deepest flesh, from the bottom of every single one of my organs. It was the scream of relief. I wasn't linked to anything anymore. I was in the immensity of air, belonging only to the birds. I was above everything. I couldn't feel my body. It was lighter than ever. I couldn't even hear myself screaming. There was nothing around me, within me. This crazy fall took my breath away, literally.

Breathe, I said to myself. *Contemplate and enjoy every second of this amazing moment. The hardest part is behind you. Look, you're falling at two hundred kilometres an hour. You still have thirty-eight seconds to savour this experience.*

I felt Eric take my hands off my harness and open my arms. Then he passed his hand under my chin to move my head up, so I could face Patrick as he filmed my fall. I felt like Superwoman. I wasn't screaming anymore; I was reborn. It was the first time in my life I was actually mindful and present, enjoying every passing second. *Carpe diem*. What a kick.

Then, we turned around for a three-sixty view. The curve of the horizon was so evident from there, and I noticed the different layers of colours in the sky. And as I went through the light clouds, there was no sound but the air buffeting me. I was still enjoying the magic when I saw Patrick waving goodbye. I waved back at him, and Eric opened our parachute. Like a powerful elastic rubber band, I flew backward. This was another amazing feeling. It was definitely worth making this dream come true. What a revelation!

The extreme sensations gave way to a relaxing moment. Everything was quiet as we descended peacefully under the parachute.

"How do you feel? How did you find it?" Eric asked.

"Oh my God. It was amazing. What a crazy jump. I thought I would never manage to breathe again after such a scream…but it all went great. It was massively impressive. What a joy it is to live this." I was happy like never before.

"You've been great, Karine," he assured me. "It's nice to sail, isn't it?"

"Oh, yeah. Now I can really relax and enjoy the ride," I said, finally unwinding.

"Tell me, do you get car sick?" he asked in a cheeky tone.

"No, I don't. Why?" I was surprised by his weird question.

"Watch."

He turned us from right to left and then gave me control of the sail, showing me how to make closer turns. The ground below me spun and twirled. I was enjoying the peace, while trying to take mental pictures of every detail of this experience, just in case it never happened again. My head was empty, without any thoughts, only focused on living every second as they came, enjoying the beautiful present my parents had offered me. I felt so lucky to be capable of facing anything. I'd jumped into the depths of the sky, and I was still flying…Until I saw the ground quickly coming towards me. It was time for the landing.

Eric had slowed us down heaps, and in three little steps, I was standing on the mainland. Patrick was already there to immortalise the moment with his video camera.

"Wow!" I said and sighed with relief.

"That was great," Patrick said, giving me a high five.

"Congrats," Eric said and kissed me on the cheek. I hugged him and gave him a friendly kiss back.

"That's a proper kiss," Eric exclaimed, giving a high five to Patrick. He didn't hide how he was flirting with me. I was flattered and happy.

"High five, guys. High five," I said, and we had another round of high-fives.

"How was it?" Patrick asked while filming my debriefing.

"A-ma-zing." I was ecstatic.

"So, tell us!" Patrick was acting like a journalist, holding his camera in front of me.

"It was incredible! Incredible! I don't know, it feels like a massive void, and then it's like *wow*." I tried to explain while laughing and mimicking my body going from standing curved in the plane to falling down into space. "It was so good. I have trouble finding the words. I still can't believe what I've just done."

"You'll come back, then?" Patrick asked.

"Oh, yes," I answered enthusiastically, even if I knew it wouldn't be right away, as my emotions were still shaken and knowing the high cost of this activity, but I had done it and really, it was a memory that would last a lifetime.

Jumping from a plane from four thousand metres high made me feel like I'd spent my entire life observing other people's adventures. It was even better than when I'd gone with my twin sister to my first concert on my twenty-fifth birthday to see the epic U2. It was a small step that helped jumpstart making my biggest dreams become a reality.

I was about to take back control of my life. I'd be jumping into space to start filling up my existence with decisions made by me. I would throw myself into a new world, a new life of my choosing, overriding my past failures. It was a small symbol for a big start over. A little death for a new life. Those four thousand metres between me and the ground had been the distance between me and the life I was dreaming of. Every single metre flown was a step closer to my forever goal—a happy life.

We walked back to the base, still talking about this incomparable experience and laughing. My parents were waiting for me, and I rushed at them to kiss them as hard as possible. I thanked them for offering me so much support and making one of my dearest dreams come true. My dad was glad to hear all about my adventures, and my mum listened with a smile.

We waited as my skydiving montage was completed, and we left once I was given the souvenir DVD. I kept a wide smile on my face until we arrived home. After we packed our stuff away, we watched the video of my skydiving experience. My dad was so happy. He was smiling and cheerful, like he hadn't been for a while. My happiness was contagious, which made me feel even better.

After dinner, I took out some pictures of the video, so my sister could measure my fall and acknowledge that I'd done the crazy jump myself. She'd also skydived, so when we chatted on the phone, she described her experience with as much enthusiasm as I was describing mine, and we laughed for a while, once again living through all these emotions together.

I also told her about Australia, and she thought it was a great idea, because having been there herself, she knew how this experience had transformed her in many positive ways. I went to bed satisfied with my day and promising myself that I would make my dreams come true this year. After a jump into space, nothing was scary anymore. I was free, and I wanted to live. I delivered my own self today. I transformed into a butterfly, and the chrysalis of my caterpillar was lying on the ground with my past. I fell asleep with a smile still on my lips.

The next day, I started to figure out how to make my Australian dream happen. I didn't lose a minute and started writing an email to my friend, to find out what kind of advice he had for me. I also asked some people on LinkedIn who were French or working in marketing in Melbourne, to give me more advice. Then I sent an email to Leslie, the lady I'd been in contact with at Internabroad, the company that was supposed to find me an internship in the U.S.A. After these quick updates, I checked my budget and the availability and price of the flight.

I wanted to leave in October with the return a year later, which was the duration of my working holiday visa. A week later, I had my flight ticket to Melbourne for October 28, 2010.

I was about to truly start living now. Then I could enjoy the rest of my life, achieving what I'd never done. After all this time taking care of others, watching over their lives, I'd forgotten my own issues, my own desires, and finally, my own life. It was time to live for myself, even if it was easier said than done. I had to be alone in a country where nobody knew me or my past, so I could build my own future.

I understood the deep mechanisms of my personality: my faults, my qualities, my behaviours and reactions, and why I was the way I was. I had high expectations to follow the principles, beliefs, and values inherited from my family. I liked my soul. I just had to become the person I was dreaming of being in this world—an accomplished woman with a career and a love life, married with kids, blooming in all aspects of society. I had the solid foundation to succeed.

5

Since my diagnosis, I find it difficult to respond when people greet me with the casual, "How are you?" It feels like a blade in my heart and seems wrong to reply, "Well, not too bad considering I have cancer." That would be awkward. So I'm keeping the secret for now. Except for the delivery team at the hospital and my family, nobody else knows. Somehow, not telling anyone makes it seem like it's not real. That I'm just in a nightmare. And I look healthy. I imagine people out there, walking in the streets, some of them having cancer, too, and I don't know. I can't see it on their faces. What a weird feeling to be dying from the inside, betrayed by my own body.

Also, I'm upset at my parents. My sister told me she would come to visit me anytime if we couldn't make the trip to France we'd planned for April, but my parents didn't even mention the eventuality of coming at all. I don't want to scream my condition to anyone, but at the same time, I'm desperate for some comfort.

I'm not looking for some kind of fake support or pity, but I do want my parents to show they care. I'd like them to tell me that I can count on them if I need anything. But they haven't, and I'm hurt. I just want to be happy for the birth of my baby. I should be excited and euphoric, and instead I'm scared of giving birth to a future orphan. But I take comfort in that I still have Justin. We're in this together, and so far, he's been quite supportive. I feel closer to him than ever before. He's always been there for me, since the day I met him, nearly five years ago.

When I landed in Melbourne on October 30, 2010, my plane had a twenty-six-hour delay, and I was exhausted but happy. As I drove in a cab to the hostel, I looked at the skyscrapers lighting the dark night. The streets were quiet, as it was already two in the morning, but I was overwhelmed by a wonderful feeling of happiness. After all these years, I was finally in Australia. My dream had come true! I felt like I could breathe for the first time in my life. I was alone in an unknown city, with not many plans and a lot of opportunities ahead of me. I was in charge of every decision, with no one telling me what to do or how to do it. I could be myself. I could try and fail. I could "waste" time finding myself. I didn't have to succeed straight away or have a "real" job.

On my first day, I woke up after only a couple of hours. The excitement was unbearable. I took my breakfast in the city centre and went to the immigration department for my working holiday visa and my Tax File Number. I also opened an Australian bank account and bought a sim card for the Aussie phone my sister had given me. In France, I would never have managed to do that in one day, but here, I got it done in three hours, and that was with taking my time. People smiled and joked with me. Even in public administrations, I was welcomed. I felt like I was in Care-Bear land, looking everywhere at everything like I'd just been given eyes.

When I created my Tax File Number on the computers at the Taxation Office, I met two Frenchies from the Alsace region who'd also wanted to start working as soon as possible. We were all surprised to have finished just in time for lunch. But it was expensive to eat properly on a tiny budget, so we went to McDonald's. Then we spent the afternoon visiting the CBD and were going downstairs after a visit to St. Patrick's Cathedral, when one of the guys broke his foot watching a beautiful girl walk away. He had to go to the hospital and get a plaster cast.

But the day went well for me. I was hired for my first job in Australia, working five hours on Wednesday for a hundred dollars, selling radios at the International Cricket Cup. I'd found the advertisement and talked with them on the phone while my mate was falling down the stairs.

We finished the day with some food shopping, but the products I was used to buying for cheap back home were quite expensive in Australia, especially fresh vegetables, and I had trouble filling up my trolley. Then I went back to my hostel and slept for twelve hours straight.

The next morning, I went to the La Trobe University offices for them to help me out with my job search, as this is where I'd received my diploma. Within ten minutes, the receptionist managed to get me a phone conversation with the marketing and communication teacher, who gave me tips and contact details for some companies that could be interested in my profile.

While I was in Melbourne, I went to Peter Pan, the coolest tour operator and Internet provider for backpackers like me, and booked my trip to Philip Island for Friday. I also took the tramway to St. Kilda, a suburb in the South of Melbourne. I wanted to end my trip close to the beach, but it was tough to find an available hostel. A Frenchie I met on the tram told me where his hostel was and that it was so difficult to find a room, because the Melbourne Cup was that weekend. Everything was booked out, but I still managed to get a bed.

The next day, I was surprised when I looked out the window. I never imagined it could rain like that. The wind was crazy strong, too.

After walking nearly six kilometres, I was drenched and freezing cold, and my umbrella didn't last long fighting the wind. I already had a cold, which didn't help my mood. But otherwise, the Melbourne Bridge was beautiful.

Afterward, I went in search of a free Wi-Fi network, as in most places I stayed it was about four dollars an hour for a slow connection. But thanks to McDonald's and libraries, I could get free access. I was at the State Library off Swanston Street with a lot of other people who'd had the same idea. I'd already booked my flight to Brisbane, as my sister told me I would love it and should stay there. I had just enough time to book my hostel and apply for a few jobs before six p.m., when the staff asked us to get out, so I hurried back to the warmth of my hostel for a well-deserved bath!

The first three days went quickly. Though the Aussies were nice and happy, my wallet was sad. But I figured I'd better to get used to it, because I loved Australia!

While enjoying a much-needed sleep-in, my French phone rang. I wondered who it could be, as everybody knew I was in Australia, and with the time difference, it was night time there, the day before. I didn't recognise the male voice straight away, and he didn't want to tell me who he was. He sounded upset and cocky, saying that I'd obviously had many other men after being with him.

That's when I realised it was my ex, François, the guy who pretty much caused a year of self-questioning and was part of the reason why I left the country. He wanted to apologise for what he'd done to me and explained that he'd been the victim of the same kind of abuser he was for me. He said he was seeing a shrink who helped him realise how much hurt he'd caused.

I was in shock. I told him I was now in Australia, no thanks to him, and asked if he had the three thousand Euros he still owed me, because that would be the best apology. But he didn't, so I hung up. With all the pain he'd caused me, I'd made myself forget his voice. Now here I was, wide awake all of a sudden. After nearly two years, he'd finally apologised, but I'd moved on.

Though he'd cheated on me, we tried to stay together, but we'd argued constantly. My discovery had opened my eyes, and I saw all the things I couldn't stand in our relationship. We'd been going nowhere but to hell. He'd been too young for me, was unemployed, and spent his days playing Xbox. I wasn't attracted to him anymore. I was angry and tired of being his mum.

After one of our many arguments, I'd told him he should move out. Then I'd had second thoughts and left him a note that I'd made a mistake. But when I rushed back home after work, thinking about the great conversation we'd have about how we needed to cut the crap and take responsibility for our actions, he was gone, having taken most of our things, including the cutlery and plates, and of course, the Xbox as well.

But I didn't want to waste any more time thinking about the past and another one of my exes. I was about to embark for a two days trip on the Great Ocean Road. We had all the weather—rain, wind, and sun—but it was amazing. I even tried the Vegemite. Yuck. I decided to stick to jam. We also tasted a typical Aussie barbecue, I saw my first koalas and kangaroos in the wild, and I fed colourful wild parrots. Wednesday, I worked selling radios at the Melbourne Cricket Ground. I had to wear a bright yellow T-shirt while carrying a yellow bag full of radios and a big yellow advertising frame above my head. What a look. It was hard, but I stayed motivated, even though again the weather was cold with showers. The match was Australia versus Sri Lanka, and it was awesome to see the supporters painted in the colours of their team. Just watching them and their excitement entertained me. I made a hundred bucks, so I was happy. After a late night, I slept in the next day and sent back eighteen kilos of winter clothes to France to avoid being in excess weight for my flight to Brisbane the next Monday.

On Friday, I went to Philip Island with another tour and visited the koala and kangaroo reserve. The best part was being able to touch the kangaroos and see koalas from a closer point of view than in the wild. Then we went to Wholemail Beach, where professional surfers had competitions if they couldn't use Bells Beach. We finished by going to the Nobbies, at the very end of Philip Island peninsula. Then we went to the beach to witness the penguin parade, where small groups of penguins doodled to the ocean to eat fish or shells they would give to their babies later. There were four lines of them, parallel to the water. One group faced the shore, while the group closest to the water fished. It was a glorious experience.

On my last weekend, I went to St. Kilda, where I visited the Botanic Garden. While discovering the flora of Australia, I imagined myself walking in these rainforests with my family and thought about how I would feel if I could live here forever…in another world, but figured it would be hard to be so far away from them.

When I landed in Brisbane on November 8, 2010, I spent two days thinking the city was lovely but not for me, because it was too far away from the beach.

On my third day, I went down to my hostel kitchen and met two French girls, Solène and Elodie, who were talking about picking capsicums in Bowen, in North Queensland. They gave me the contact details of the farmer, and within the hour, I managed to get a job. I made sure I was paid hourly, not by the bucket, and booked my flight and accommodation to stay with the girls. They seemed nice, and I was happy to leave Brisbane with a job and two new friends. We arrived in Bowen the same night, around nine o'clock. Bowen Wood was the place where they filmed the movie *Australia*, and I stayed at the hotel where some scenes had been filmed.

I loved this movie, because it made me dream of seeing these magnificent landscapes, deserted but green. But I was living in a sort of ghost town, cut by large dirt streets and shaped by low one-storey buildings, where the population density was near one for a square kilometre. A sort of Wild West kind of place, where men were the majority, and there was alcohol for all. The main activity consisted of going to the bar in the hotel I was staying at. There was a nice outdoor area where the music, neither current nor country, echoed up to my bedroom, until late at night. Here, men and a few women lived on the rhythm of the work in the field. They'd go to sleep and wake up early. I had to get used to it quickly, as the next morning I would start picking at six.

It was tough at first, but the day was so exhausting that I was in bed by nine anyway. This first day was the same as the following ones. I'd wake up at five and put on my combat outfit, an old pair of pants and t-shirt, because this job was so dirty that I had to take two showers at night, until the water stopped being brown. Then we'd all jump into a thirty-seater bus to reach the farm, a sort of big shed in the middle of the fields, in the beautiful Aussie outback.

The trip was short but rocky on the dirt road damaged by the mud. The girls were pretty happy about this adventure, and I had to admit that when I realised the kind of transportation we'd be taking to reach the field, I got quite excited. We climbed the back platform of a big truck where eight big red bins of about a cubic metre were placed, and jumped into one of them. We could seat four to a bin. I felt like a clandestine immigrant hiding while crossing the border. Then once the truck stopped, we jumped off quickly to go into our field.

There was nothing else but working lands in this flat landscape. The air was warm and humid. Green covered most of the ochre lands of an Australia I hadn't been introduced to yet. The fields were split by long lines full of capsicums trees. Each of us got five to six buckets and took a line where we placed them every two metres.

Then we started picking, following the boss's directions. He was Turkish and macho, with limited English composed of action sentences and some, "Hey, Boy", "Hey, girl", "Go there", "Two lines", "More buckets", "Stop talking", and "Faster," thrown in, all with a strong accent that rolled the letter "R." I was definitely an immigrant, paid to do a job in the middle of the poisonous cane toads and brown snakes, the second deadliest snake in the world, with a bite that kills in twenty minutes, leaving no time to reach a hospital.

The heat and the sun burned me all day, but the farmer wouldn't let us go back to our stuff at the end of the field so we could put on sunscreen, since it was a waste of productivity. As a result, my fair skin got sunburned. I almost got fired one day, because I couldn't stand the burn any longer and had to apply cream on my skin. This hot weather made the task even more painful. We usually finished at 4:30 or five p.m., that is, when our driver didn't forget us, because he was at the pub.

I was happy in the fields, though, listening to music and trying to keep smiling despite the aches in my body. After six days, we had a day off, because it was raining. That morning, I couldn't get out of bed, because I was way too sore. We waited for the next day to get our pay and finally left, because the rainy season had started a month early. It would just get worse, with no guarantee of work, and the hostel still required two hundred bucks a week. It wasn't worth it.

I decided to leave with two French guys, Max and Christian, who lived in my hotel. They were going on a road trip to Sydney by car. I hadn't planned on visiting there, but why not? I'd always wanted to go on a road trip, so I joined them. We left the girls, knowing that we would spend New Year's Eve in Sydney, which was famous for its fireworks.

We left on the evening of Friday, November 19, 2010 for ten days of adventure. We set up a tent and slept at Airlie Beach. The next day, we went to the rainforest in Finch Hatton Gorge and walked across four rivers and five kilometres under the rain, which I guess is the best way to enjoy the rainforest. Then we planted the tent in Eungella National Park, near Rainbow Beach, where the light of the moon reflected on the white sand of the Park. It was magical.

We also went for a walk in Great Sandy National Park, in the forest. We got lost and walked over twenty kilometres, most of them along Rainbow Beach, but we still enjoyed the beauty of one of Australia's most beautiful beaches. What I loved the most about this trip was our great spontaneity without any timeframe. Even when we got lost, we still made some interesting discoveries and had no choice but to be in the moment. The same night, we drove to Noosa and tried to sleep on the beach, but the rain brought us back to the car. Sleeping in the seats wasn't easy, but at least we were dry.

The sun came back the next morning, perfect for us to enjoy the beach and my first surf session. Till Tree Beach felt like I was in a washing machine before I finally managed to sit on my board to wait for a wave. This first time was exciting but difficult on a small, pointy board.

After some food shopping and a well-deserved barbecue, we drove to Caloundra, a lovely city on the beach, and went to the lighthouse before sleeping in the car again.

In the morning we went to the Glass House Mountains. The hike was steep, and the rain surprised us. We had just enough time to get undercover in a limestone cave before the storm. Half an hour later, the sun came back, and we finished climbing the high hill. It was a sacred summit for the Aboriginals, and I could see why. The landscape was mesmerising, with green as far as the eye could see. There were sixteen summits, all different shapes and sizes, some red from the rocks, and some green from the grass, trees, and plants.

After contemplating the beautiful three-sixty view, rich in humidity and life, we walked back down and had a nice noodle picnic with the flies before hitting the road again to King's beach, where I had my second surf session. I got better at it, but standing on the board was still a challenge.

The next day, we drove south to Brisbane, where we jumped on the Internet Wi-Fi to update our friends and family about our lives and went for a jug of beer with two of the boys' mates. In the evening, we were back on the road to Byron Bay and managed to sleep on the beach, as finally there was no rain. The sunrise was beautiful. I watched the dance of the dolphins on the horizon, a hot coffee in my hand. Then I tried another surf session but quit right away. My body was exhausted, beaten by the waves and pulled by the currents, my surfboard leached to my left foot. We rested on the beach, where we spent another night.

On Saturday, we arrived in Nimbin after a forty-kilometre drive through the country. It was a city where hippies and all sorts of artists lived like they were trapped in the seventies. As I walked around the two main streets, this little joyful town made me feel like time had stopped. We found psychedelic décors and were offered marijuana cookies, as well as magic mushrooms and weed. They also had a "Mardi Grass" fair, a sort of peaceful manifestation for marijuana legalisation.

After a couple of stops along the road, we finally arrived in the largest Australian city, Sydney, on the first of December. We couldn't park in the city, because it was way too expensive, so we found a hostel in Glebe, where we could park for free. Then we spent the next three days looking for a job using the free library Wi-Fi and walking the streets of the city centre to dispatch our resumes. By Sunday, the girls from Bowen, Solène and Elodie, had joined us, and we all enjoyed a day out at Bondi Beach, walking along the beautiful coastal path to Coogee Beach. It was nice to be back at the sand and surf after three days in the city, even if the ocean water was freezing.

The following week, I spent my first days looking for a job with Solène, I already had some leads and had passed two trials, so I went to the Aquarium Museum with the boys on Friday.

I took my Responsible Service of Alcohol (RSA) training that Saturday. I needed it in order to serve alcohol at a pub or restaurant in New South Wales, where alcohol was everywhere, even though it was expensive, and it seemed like a lot of people had issues with alcoholism. If anything happened to a customer who drank too much, I could get fined up to $5,500 dollars and even go to jail. At least the teacher was really funny. I felt like I was at a comedy club, as he had a true story for each subject we studied. Even with his strong Aussie accent, I managed to understand everything and passed it easily after paying the required fifty bucks. Anyway, it looked like anybody could pass as long as they paid. It was all about business, I guessed.

On Sunday, I woke up early to go surfing with the boys at Maroubra Bay. I was getting better, but I also got a bad sunburn. Here, after half an hour, you could get burnt, even with sunscreen. I've never seen that before. I went to the chemist to get some ointment to soothe my skin, and he freaked me out by telling me that after three sunburns, you could get cancer. He went on to say that here in Australia, the sun was different, and I had to be careful. I'd been sunburned so many times in my life, but even more since I was here, with picking and all.

On Monday, I wanted to make sure I had the two jobs I'd been accepted for, as my bosses should have called me on Friday but didn't. So I woke up at 7:30 a.m. to go to the AB Hotel in Glebe first and then to The Good Co. Café in the city. It was good news. I found out I would start the next morning at the café, from seven a.m. to twelve p.m., Monday through Friday, and at the pub on Friday nights. I was happy to finally be integrated into the society. Even if it wasn't my dream job, it was a start, and I could really improve my English.

The Good Co. Café was located in the NAB bank building on George Street in the city centre. It was always full and was the fifth most productive café in the city.

The AB Hotel was one of the oldest pubs in Sydney, located on Glebe Point Road, ten minutes away from our share house. I was definitely living the life of a normal Sydney sider. We'd found a nice townhouse with two bathrooms, where we could all fit. Solène and I shared the bedroom upstairs. Christian and Max shared a room downstairs, and we also had two Aussie students who were brothers, in another two bedrooms upstairs. The house was renovated and nice, especially after living all my life in a flat. There was a great backyard, internet, and all bills were included. I decided to stay until my planned trip to Thailand with the girls in February.

I was working and making money while sacrificing on food to pay the hundred and fifty dollars a week in rent. This meant I could save heaps, something I hadn't been able to do in France, for sure. It was so easy to save money here. Sydney was more hectic, dynamic, and modern than Melbourne, but I loved the food and the kindness of the people, and could see myself living there. Also, the job research would definitely be easier than back home.

Life was simpler in so many ways. Except for the two regulars at the pub who always complained because I was French, and that a real Aussie would pour their beer better, in general, people were generous, easy-going and honest. What a change. Back home, I'd been so depressed by people never smiling, barely acknowledging me, and always complaining about how terrible their life was. Don't get me wrong. All this negativity was so contagious, I'd become one of them, and I hated it. In Australia, it was like I was on another planet. People gave me a chance. They didn't judge me straight away. They tried to get to know me as another human being and not only in order to get something from me. Overall, they were less defensive, argumentative, or confrontational, and more generous, charitable, and helpful. In a nutshell, more …human.

My daily routine was to wake up at five a.m., get ready, and take the bus to the CBD. I would arrive at the café at seven a.m. and start preparing my work zone for the morning. About two hundred slices of toasted bread and spread later, I would finish at 11:30 a.m.

I came to realise how Australia was such a coffee society. People here took their coffee experience to a whole new level that I wasn't used to. Like many French people, I loved my morning espresso, but it was rare to see someone adding milk, or syrups. After working at the café, I'd get a bite to take away and rush to catch the bus back to Glebe. Then I'd go home and take a nap for an hour before walking to the pub, where I'd be from around two p.m. until late at night, cleaning, serving, and talking to my customers.

After a couple of months, I passed my RCG, a certificate required to work in the gaming room. I loved it, not only because of my noon to six p.m. schedule, which meant I got my evenings back, but also because it was more about customer service. The only drawback was that it was dark in there, and I missed the light of the day. Also, all the noises were painful to deal with at first. I never gambled. We didn't have gambling machines back home, except in casinos, so I didn't really understand how some people could become so addicted to it. Once a guy threw his stool into the machine's screen, because he lost big money. It freaked me out.

On a Thursday in January, I was working behind the bar, when a guy came up to the counter. He was of average size, with wide shoulders and muscled calves. He wore the yellow shirts that labourers and tradies wore. In France, these people were devalued, yet here he was, smiling and seemingly happy.

"G'day," he said. "Can I have a VB, please?"

"We don't have VB. Maybe you'd like something else?" I asked after checking in the fridges. I was a little dismayed I couldn't give him what he wanted.

"Oh, I'm sure you've got VBs in the bottle shop. Can you please have a look?"

Okay. Now this guy was getting under my skin, and I found his behaviour nearly rude, telling me how to do my job. But I went to the bottle shop anyway to check it out…and found it. I came back to the bar a bit confused.

He took it happily. I couldn't believe he didn't seem upset by my short attitude. Maybe it wasn't that bad if he didn't notice anything. After all, I stayed polite the whole time. When I went to the till and looked up the price, I found it in the bottle shop section and asked for the payment.

"It's four dollars please."

"I think you gave me the bottle shop price. You have to add the pub fee."

Oh my God, this guy was so honest. In France, nobody would have told me I made a mistake. I was shocked and confused, but I looked it up and discovered he was correct.

"I guess you should work here," I said. "You're right again. It will be six dollars, please," I said with a cheeky grin.

He smiled and thanked me as he handed over the money. "And that's for you," he said, giving me another two bucks. Then he took his beer and left to find a seat in the smoking area.

What had I just witnessed? Not only was he nice about the entire situation, but generous, giving me a 30 percent tip. No one had ever given me such a tip at the bar. Okay, I received a lucky fifty-dollar note at the café on my first day, but otherwise people rarely tipped.

With time, I came to realise he was a regular who came every Thursday. And when I started working downstairs in the gaming room, where my boss put VB on tap, he was happy to come and chat a few minutes with me. After a couple of times, he finally introduced himself.

His name was Justin, and he thought I was Swedish, certainly because of my blond hair and blue eyes. He was surprised to learn that I was French, because he didn't think I had the typical French accent.

When I'd started working at the pub back in December, I'd met James, a tall Aussie bloke with light blue eyes and messy dark hair. He'd come in regularly with his mates and was always flirtatious and smiley to me. He had a kangaroo in a triangle tattooed on his back, so I nicknamed him "Kangaroo." But after a few dates, I figured it wasn't going anywhere. He was rude, unreliable, and such a player. He gambled and drink too much for my liking and was also jealous. He didn't trust me if I socialised without him. We'd argue a lot, and I couldn't stand it anymore. After three weeks of dating, we hadn't seen or contacted each other for a week, and I thought it was over. But then he came to the pub on the last Thursday of January to see me, followed by his mates, a jug of beer in hand.

He asked how I was and called me babe, acting nonchalant, when I'd been in shutdown mode for a week, raging that he couldn't care less about not seeing me.

They played the rest of the afternoon, and when I told him I couldn't drink at the pub in my uniform, he told me to go get changed, and they'd wait for me. But when I got back twenty minutes later, they were gone. After looking everywhere and trying to contact him many times on his mobile, he sent me a text asking me to meet him at his place.

Justin was about to leave, when we both reached the door at the same time.

He asked me if I was okay, and I replied, "I guess."

Then he said I could join him and his mates for a beer, but I declined.

"Thank you very much," I said. "It would be great, but my boyfriend just let me down again, and I really need to tell him it's over face to face. I don't want to let this go like that."

"You should be treated like a princess. Maybe next time, then. Good luck," he said.

I took the bus to James' place, and after another disappointing night, I left him for good. Then I spent a lonely week working my arse off and jogging in the park, while trying to enjoy nights out with my mates. I was more upset than sad, so once I got over my frustrations, I got over him. In this difficult time, I missed my sister a lot. My family and friends, too, but I wasn't ready to go home. I loved my life in Australia and wanted to stay. I felt like maybe going back home for the holidays would be nice, but not forever. Not yet, anyway.

Two weeks after my breakup with Kangaroo, I saw Justin.

"So that's it?" he asked in a shy voice. "You and James are officially over?"

"Yes. I'm done with it. He was driving me crazy."

"He didn't deserve to be with someone like you, anyway."

"I should be treated like a princess, right?"

"Exactly." He gave me a smile and left for the smoking area.

Then he came to see me for another two rounds, each time more chatty and smiley.

When he came back a third time, and I gave him his VB, he said "Do you like coffee?"

"Of course, I like coffee. I'm French."

"I was wondering," he said. "Would you like to go for a coffee with me, maybe on Sunday morning?" He asked this knowing we both worked six days a week.

"A coffee? On Sunday morning? Like for breakfast?" I asked, surprised that for once, someone hadn't asked me out for a drink, at night.

"Yes, I just would like to know you better. Don't worry, no expectations," he said, probably thinking I'd just come out of a disappointing story, and he didn't want to start anything just yet.

"Yes, why not? No expectations, right?"

I found a pen for him to write down his number. At this moment, I had an intuition that I would never call him, and. I didn't want to miss out on happiness, just because he wasn't my type. He had lovely hazelnut eyes and seemed genuine and honest. He was always nice to me and behaved as a gentleman. After all, he'd said there were "no expectations," and I felt like I could trust him.

"You know what? I'm going to give you my number," I said with a grin. "Because to be honest, if you give me yours, I'll never call you."

"Okay…I'm not sure how I should take that," he replied, a bit confused.

"Don't worry," I said. "It's better for you. I never call when guys give me their number, and I'd like to go for a coffee and get to know you. So, please, take my number and call me, okay?"

I gave him my mobile number, and he left happy, a big smile on his face. Also, he'd probably had a couple of beers to find the strength to ask me out.

On Sunday morning, we were supposed to meet by eleven a.m. at the World Centre on George Street, but Justin arrived at nearly one in the afternoon. He'd called earlier to let me know he'd be late, and I didn't mind anyway. When he arrived, I barely recognised him in his "civilian" clothes: a pair of jeans, a shirt, and casual shoes. He'd also cut his hair and shaved his light beard. That's why he was late. He'd been at the hairdresser. A red rose in hand and a smile on his face, he came towards me. It was nice to see he'd gone out of his way to impress me.

"Hello. Sorry I'm late. That's for you," he said, offering me the flower. "I wanted to make a good first impression for our first date. But no expectations…" He grinned at me.

"No expectations at all." I smiled back at him, flattered that he considered this a date.

Since I'd already had a lot of coffee, I suggested going for a beer instead, so we went a pub with an above-ground terrace about a hundred metres away.

We spent about two hours chatting about our lives. It was so easy to talk to him, but I noticed my English wasn't as good as I thought, because I could barely understand him, except for when he asked me if I wanted another beer. He was swallowing his words and speaking with lots of slang. He had to repeat some sentences as he struggled to understand my French accent.

He seemed pretty interested in what I was saying. At least he was listening. He also sprang for two beers for me without blinking, and that was a nice change. We laughed and didn't stop chatting. It was so easy to be comfortable with him, and he made me feel special. He paid attention and looked at me like I shone.

After two and half hours, it was time for me to go to Town Hall station to catch up with Tani, my Scottish friend from Melbourne. We'd planned to do a pub crawl that day, since I'd broken up with Kangaroo. I'd never done one before, and I wanted to experience it. Justin walked me to the station. Tani was late, but Justin stayed with me the entire forty-five minutes, chatting and telling me how he preferred to be with a beautiful girl like me rather than going home to his brother. He was so sweet and a true gentleman.

That's how we started dating. During the week, he'd pick me up after my shift at the pub, and we'd go for a couple of drinks in another pub up the street. On Sundays, he'd show me around Sydney. At the end of February, we went to the Chinese Garden and Darling Harbour for our fifth date, and we finally had our first kiss, a quick one at my front door when he dropped me off.

On the next date, three days later, we were all fire and passion. But I wanted to use my Grandma Denise's advice: he had to wait. I wouldn't be easy prey. He needed to seduce and court me, like a gentleman. Though he already was one, always holding doors open for me, complimenting me, listening to me, and picking me up and dropping me off at home. I was happy.

He was so different from the guys I'd dated before. He was patient and sweet. He had such a great heart, always so positive and happy. I learned a lot about him, and we got better at understanding each other. He even downloaded a dictionary app on his phone, so he could write down words I didn't understand and get the French translation for it. He was caring and affectionate with me. The way he looked at me made me feel so special. I trusted him.

We spoke so much about our lives and everything else, that after seven dates I felt like I'd known him all my life. He told me that I pretty much knew him better than anyone else did.

Justin was a happy thirty-two-year-old labourer, who spent most of his time working. He'd left his hometown, Wollongong, at sixteen to work in Sydney. And it was only recently that he'd started living with his younger brother, Jay, and his Italian mum, so they could afford to rent a better place in the expensive city.

His childhood was spent in housing and commission, raised by young parents who ended up separating. He'd also been cared for by his grandmother and step-grandfather for a while. He never met his mum's dad, as his Italian grandma left him after they arrived in Australia with their six kids. His step-grandfather, Jack, was a war hero and father figure, and Justin had lots of admiration for the man.

When he was fourteen, he stopped going to school, because his teacher told him not to sit in the front row if he wanted to stay in class. He was trying to do the right thing, and the teacher thought he was insolent. But he knew that if he remained at the back, he wouldn't learn and would be distracted.

He used to date a lot, and he nearly got engaged, thinking it was what she wanted. It wasn't. He used to not believe in friendship, because he said friends always disappointed you, but now he had a nice group of mates. He was such a beautiful soul. He'd been hurt badly by family and friends. I had, too, and somehow we were together against the world.

He introduced me to some of his mates when he took me to a barbecue. There, I met a French bloke who was married to an Aussie. Like me, he loved Australia and wanted to stay all his life there, even after only a couple of months. Talking to him, I realised how I would love to stay my entire life. I enjoyed the cosmopolitan aspect of this amazing country, the various cultures, and everyone bringing to the table their own traditions, where everything seemed possible.

I loved how the small business and the economy in general was managed, and also the way they still understood the human side of things. There was a community spirit, something that didn't really exist in France. It was wonderful the way they used any occasion to party and how they'd catch up or meet at the pub. They were so optimistic. Everything was different, from the opposite seasons, the flora and fauna, and the driving on the left side, to the wide-open space and houses, versus overcrowded streets and tiny flats. Even the moon looked different.

Of course, everything went well, and this barbecue was another good time spent with Justin. He'd never introduced any of his girlfriends to the people in his life before, which made me feel even more special. Things seemed to be a bit more serious for him, but I hadn't wanted to rush into anything. We spent our first month together sending affectionate text messages and beautiful love quotes to each other. Justin was hard to compete with.

6

I spend the rest of my week going to hospital for various appointments.

Tuesday. I see my obstetrician for my first injection of steroids, so the baby's lungs can start to open. Also, I have an ultrasound to see how big the baby is. It's so painful to think that because of me, he or she will greet the world earlier than expected. But apparently since they now weigh two and a half kilograms, they should be big enough to avoid the NICU. The technician is nice and shows me the baby in three dimensions. She even gives me some printouts, which makes me think it's a girl for sure. She has voluptuous lips.

Wednesday. Second injection of steroids.

On Thursday, Justin and I go to see my new surgeon, who specialises in melanoma, at the Poche Centre in Crows Nest, an hour's drive away from home. He tells us that if I felt a lump back in July, that the melanoma started at least six months previous. So I'm already nine months in. He's still thinking the cancer is only at stage III, so we're both hoping it hasn't spread to other organs yet. Otherwise, it could be a lot worse. He doesn't want to talk about this option and prefers to let me know that at stage III, they perform a surgery to get rid of all the cancerous lymph nodes. He also reassures me that having my baby at thirty-six weeks should be fine, because it's only a few days before full term.

So the plan is for me to give birth on October twenty-sixth. After that, I will have a PET scan on the thirtieth to make sure I don't have other tumours elsewhere. And then finally, I will have the surgery on November third. He also adds that if they saw three tumours at the ultrasound, there were more than likely twenty of them underneath. I'm terrified. He seems to think they're localised only under my armpit. I'm hoping so.

On our way back home, I check online, and Dr. Google tells me that the odds of living beyond five years with a stage III melanoma are only 20 percent…but my eyes get blurry when looking at the horrific 5 percent prognosis at stage IV. I'm just hoping we'll get rid of it with the operation, and that with treatment, it will never come back again. I can't help but think about Justin and the life he'll have if I'm not here to help him with the babies. I'm trying to stay strong and positive for them and am living every day as it comes, finding some joy in thinking about welcoming my beautiful baby into the world.

Thank goodness they won't have to suffer the circumstances of their birth. I need to be happy and enjoy the moment, like the day we welcomed Jack into our life. It was a tough one as well, but it's such a beautiful memory.

On October twenty-sixth, a beautiful baby will be born, healthy and perfect. It's weird to know the birthday already. They will be a Scorpio, a water sign. Justin, being a Taurus, is an Earth sign. Jack is a Gemini, so he's air, and I'm a Leo, so I'm fire. We will have the four elements, a perfect combination for our family. I pray that I have a girl who looks like me, so they'll remember me somehow. It sounds selfish, but I can't help it. I also hope Justin will be able to cope with everything at home, on top of our young children. I want to stay alive for them, or at least until they're old enough to be independent, because Jack and these children will need their mum for a while.

If there's a God up there, I'm praying so hard for a beautiful and easy baby girl. She will be my rock, since she's sharing this cancer journey with me from the beginning. I've already relied on this baby to find strength and positive thoughts. Justin and I even agreed on a name: Elyze.

One night, I asked him to stop everything for half an hour. So there we were, lying in bed, looking at the ceiling and saying names out loud, brainstorming. At first, he wasn't keen on Elise. He thought it would be nice with a Y, and I wanted a Z so it could be pronounced the French way. And that was it. Like for Jack, we only have one name, so it has to be a girl. The good thing about having an inducement is that I don't have to do my progesterone treatment anymore or avoid intimacy, because after all, if the baby wants to arrive naturally, it will be even better.

Friday, I have lunch with my workmates. I haven't been at the office, but it's my official last day. And since I missed out again on the baby shower they usually do, they were nice enough to organise a lunch in Botany Bay, at an Italian restaurant not too far from my place. We don't talk about my health, since only two of them are aware, and it's nice to focus on the flowers and presents, chatting about the last ultrasound, and showing off the three-dimensional print-out of my maybe daughter. Everyone has a guess as to the gender, and I'm glad to find out that only one of them thinks it could be a boy. We have a good time laughing and joking about parenthood, and soon it's time for me to leave.

I have to go to the maternity ward at St. George's hospital to see my obstetrician and plan the birth details. Then I'll go back there on Sunday at three p.m. before it begins at six p.m. Justin and Jack will have a room in the paediatric ward, so Justin will be with me for the delivery, while Jack is under the nurse's supervision. It's such a nice gesture, since we don't have any family to take care of our son, and I feel better knowing that Jack will see the baby straight after the delivery. Since it's so close to term this time, we should be able to take them home. And though it's unlikely the baby will have cancer, the placenta will still be sent for examination to be sure.

I'm trying to rest before the birth of my baby Scorpio, because I'll need all my energy and strength. I'll have to take care of a newborn and a seventeen-month-old child while having my cancer treatment. I'm praying with everything in my soul for my baby every night and that it will all go well. I'm also asking for mercy for Justin, Jack and me, after the most beautiful five years I've ever had in my life. My time has been too short for it to be over so quickly. I weep when I remember how I thought about leaving this world five years ago, before I departed my country for good. I don't want that anymore, ever. I have everything to live for now, and everything to lose.

I remember when Justin and I fell in love. We'd only been dating a month. It all started with a weekend away in the Blue Mountains.

Justin wanted to show me the Blue Mountains and organised a trip for us. He knew that no one had ever done this for me before. It was a coincidence that this weekend fell on our one-month anniversary, but I was glad about that and thought it was a sweet gesture. We also hadn't been intimate with each other up until this point. It had been my call, and I was so glad, because as a result, our relationship was more intense. Things were getting warmer between us, and we were like two teenagers falling for one another. Of course, this first weekend would be special, the next step in our relationship. Also, I was excited to see this part of New South Wales, as my sister told me it was beautiful. I had a cold, but nothing would take away the magic of this trip.

He picked me up early, and after a stop at a café for some takeaway beverages, we drove for two hours, chatting about the activities we'd would do once we got there.

We arrived in front of the magical Three Sisters in Katoomba that appeared slowly underneath the morning fog coming from the rainforest underneath. We contemplated the view and took some pictures to immortalise the moment. Then we walked in the rainforest and got closer to one of the three rocks. It was beautiful. Later, we went to the local RSL Club for a beer and a quick bite while waiting to check in. I didn't know what an RSL Club was, so Justin explained that at one time it was a place where war veterans met, but now everyone could attend and get cheaper prices than in a local pub.

At two p.m., we dropped our bags at the hotel, which was country style and a bit kitsch, but comfortable. We left the room quickly to visit the area, and we hit all the tourist attractions. We took the Sky View, a sort of cable railway going across the valley, offering a glass-bottom panorama of the beauty of the Blue Mountains, including the Three Sisters and the beautiful Katoomba falls, with their over two-hundred-metre drop. It was short but impressive. Then we walked to the bottom of the falls to have a closer look, and Justin told me he loved waterfalls and fireworks just like I did.

We took pictures and again strolled through the rainforest. He helped me walk across the river on the stones, discovering the beautiful landscapes of the Blue Mountains and the valley covered in a dense green forest. I love rides, and I was so glad he took me to the steepest train in the world. There was a fifty-two-degree incline with a fast drop down to the valley. It was awesome. We also went up to the coal mine.

Then we realised it was already five o'clock and time to go if we didn't want to walk all the way back to the top of the mountains. So we jumped on board the last train and went for a beer in a local pub, where there was a mesmerising view of the mountains surrounding us. We talked for more than an hour. It was so relaxing being there with him.

When the sun was slowly setting, we snuggled up together and watched the sky change from blue to pink and then bright orange, and the mountains turn different shades of blue, depending on how far away they were. I felt closer to Justin than ever. He'd been a true gentleman all day, satisfying my thirst for discovery and adventure. I don't think he realised how touched I was by his kind gesture of a wonderful weekend, and most importantly, the company of a generous and romantic guy. He had such a good heart and he was so patient with me. I'd never encountered a person like him.

We went back to the RSL Club for dinner, as the best restaurant in town was fully booked. Justin seemed a bit disappointed. I didn't care, as long as we were together, but after a basic dinner, I realised why he'd been so upset. Afterward, we sat by the dance floor, with me on Justin's lap, and watched an old couple dancing a waltz.

"I love to watch these old people," he said. It's so beautiful. They've been married for such a long time, yet they seem so happy. Check out the way they look at each other."

"You're right, it's beautiful. My parents used to argue so much when I was growing up, that I sometimes wonder if they would have divorced if my mum hadn't had her stroke. These guys make it look so easy to be happy forever."

"Yes, they do," he said. But I'm sure if you find the right person, you can also be happy forever."

"Yeah, probably."

We gazed into each other's eyes with intensity, and a long kiss followed. Then I asked, "Do you want to go to play the pokies (poker machines)?"

"Do you play them?" he replied, surprise in his voice.

"No, I don't. But you're going to teach me."

I had some basic knowledge, thanks to my RCG. We went to the gaming room, where I picked a machine with lions on the front. As I was a Leo, I thought it could bring me good fortune and that my favourite animal would sort me out. I put a two-dollar coin into the slot, and we played for a couple of hours. Justin couldn't believe it. We talked about anything and everything while he tried to explain to me how the lines worked. I won nearly thirty dollars, and I insisted on paying for another round of beers for once. We laughed a lot and had so much fun. It had been such a long time since I'd felt that good with a man and could totally be myself. Though I'd had beginner's luck at the poker machines, I felt even luckier having this man in my life.

Then, we went back to the hotel. The time to sleep in the same bed had come. I felt like a teenager, excited and shy, confused and anxious. But though we shared some passionate kisses and caresses, we decided to stop and fell asleep soon after, in each other arms.

We woke up the next morning, a bit tired, and went for a coffee on the main street of Katoomba, where we spoke about what happened the night before. I didn't want him feeling uncomfortable all day, and most of all, needed him to know that I wasn't making a big deal out of it.

Then we drove to the Victoria Falls, but once there, we realised we'd have to walk for six hours to see the actual falls, so we gave up and enjoyed the beauty of the valley. He made me drive his car on the dirt road. I knew how to operate a manual car on the right side of the road, with the wheel on the left, but it was weird having it be the other way around. It was also uncomfortable using my left hand for the manual gearbox, as I'm right-handed. But I did pretty well for my first time, and we laughed a lot, Justin joked about how I was a blonde woman, driving on the wrong side of the road. I couldn't blame him. I thought the same.

We drove seventy-five more kilometres to the Jenolan Caves, but the rain was pouring down when we reached the magnificent place, so we couldn't visit the cave we wanted. Instead, we went for a walk in the biggest one that was above-ground and accessible to everyone. It was close to a stream, and we decided to follow it. We were like two adventurers. The rain was just a drizzle by this point, and we could walk without being drenched.

The stream brought us once again into the rainforest, where we walked past a nineteenth-century dam and lots of dragon lizards. It was beautiful, and we were happy to be there, laughing and poking at each other, enjoying the décor and each other's company.

After the dam, a beautiful waterfall gave way to a nice little lake. And as the sun came back, a rainbow formed above the waterfall. It was magical. Lizards were everywhere, and there was no one else around. It was just the two of us in this amazing landscape. We took some pictures up close, now so comfortable and happy together. Finally, we went back to the car, and I felt something tickling at my ankles. I mentioned it to Justin, and he became unsettled.

"Quick, show me."

I showed him my feet, and he rubbed my ankles.

"What is it?" I asked, getting worried.

"Leeches. Look all over you. Shake your feet, and check your shoes and pants. You need to take them off before they suck your blood," he said calmly, as if it were the most normal thing in the world.

"Whaaat?" I said, panicking. "Leeches? Oh my God." I made sure to take off everything he'd asked me to and removed any I saw.

"It's fine. The bloody suckers aren't that bad. Don't worry. I had one or two on my own ankles. Just make sure you don't have any more, and we can go. I don't really want you to jump while I'm driving." He laughed.

"Haha, very funny," I said. "I'm not that scared. Come on. Anyway, I thought they'd be bigger, from what my sister had told me."

It was time to leave the sunset and the Blue Mountains behind us. After stopping for fuel and a quick sandwich, it was nearly night time when we reached Sydney.

I smiled and said, "Can we stop by your place? I'd like to stay a bit longer with you tonight."

We watched a movie together on his couch and made love for the first time that night. It was a sweet, passionate, affectionate, and tender moment, full of loving cuddles. Then we had a shower together in each other's arms and enjoyed the hot water running on our shoulders.

"I had a very nice time with you this weekend," I said.

"Me, too," he replied and kissed me on my forehead. Then he said, "…Karine?"

"Yes?"

"Can I ask you if you want to be my girlfriend now?"

"I already am." I laughed. "From the moment we kissed each other, I considered you my boyfriend. In France, we don't date."

"How come?"

"If you kiss someone and see them regularly, you shouldn't be with anyone else. You're supposed to be exclusive straight away."

"Really?" he said. "That's weird."

"No, I think the other way around is weird. If you choose to be with someone, you shouldn't kiss or sleep with anybody else. Have you gone out with anyone since you started dating me?"

"No, I haven't. I was seeing someone before you, but I stopped after our first date."

"Oh, really? That's fine, I guess." I shrugged. "So, this entire dating thing isn't that great. I mean, if you find someone interesting, you really don't have to see anybody else at the same time."

"Can I tell you something?" He hesitated.

"Of course. What is it?"

"I'm not sure if it's the right time… it may be a bit too early." He seemed awkward all of a sudden.

"It's okay. You can tell me later." I said, thinking he wanted to say those three big words. Even if I was falling for him, I wasn't ready to say it yet.

He drove me home, even though I could tell he wanted to stay together. However, we both had work the next day.

Justin and I spent the next two months seeing each other as much as we could, despite our busy schedules. I was working fifty hours a week, so we really had only a couple of nights together and Sundays. He guided me around Sydney, taking me to the north coast of Bondi beach, with its fish and chips shops on the harbour, and Centennial Park, with its black swans and ducks swimming on beautiful lakes and trees full of bats. I spent most of my Saturday nights at his place, and we loved waking up on Sunday morning in each other's arms.

On the last Sunday of March, he introduced me to his dad, Stephen. I was a bit anxious, as he'd never been all that positive about his relationship with the man. His dad lived in a housing and commission house in Maroubra, a Sydney suburb close to the beach. His German Shepard dog barked just as we were about to enter.

His place was dirty with stuff everywhere and smelled of dog. There was dog hair everywhere, and I felt uncomfortable, even though his dad welcomed me with a big smile and a cup of tea. He was skinny yet toned, average size, in pretty good shape for his age, but his face was aged and full of wrinkles. His hair was blond and long and worn in a ponytail.

I sat on the edge of an old and dirty couch and tried to keep up appearances. Justin and his dad spoke in English, but I could barely understand their conversation. It was way too fast for me. I did manage to understand that he thought I was pretty. There was a lot of slang and familiar Aussie language in their conversation, so I gave up and looked around. The house was in bad shape, and his dad appeared to be a bit of a hoarder. He seemed nice but poor and not attached to cleanliness. I couldn't help remembering what Justin had said about him and his troubled past.

I had trouble breathing in this atmosphere, and the situation made me feel even more uncomfortable. What a petty, arrogant Frenchie I was, thinking that way. It was the reason I'd left France; all those people judging a book by its cover. I thought that if Justin was his son, at least he'd done one thing right, and I didn't want to punish my boyfriend for his "old man." I was with Justin, not his father. I didn't choose my parents, and neither did he. My *gentleman*, as I called him, didn't seem to notice my discomfort, just that I was quiet. At some point, I had to ask when we would leave, so he'd get the hint. I was happy to get some fresh air and decided to leave this awkward experience aside for now. I didn't want to ruin a potential love story because of his family.

The next weekend, while I spent the night at Justin's place after our usual movie night, he got sick. We were lying in bed, and he began shaking with fever. I was so worried, because he'd always been so strong and fearless.

"What's wrong?" I asked.

"Nothing. I'm okay. It's okay," he said, still shaking.

"I'm sorry, you're not okay. You're boiling hot, and you're shivering. Please tell me what's wrong."

"I don't want to talk to you about it." He sounded weird.

"Come on, what is it? You can trust me."

"It's going to be fine, don't worry." He was in a weird foetal position.

"Okay, I'm starting to get upset now. Tell me what's going on."

"It's just that…I've got haemorrhoids, and it's getting worse…" he said, a bit embarrassed.

"Are you kidding me?" I laughed. "Really. That's what you didn't want to tell me?" I couldn't stop laughing.

"It's not funny. I'm in terrible pain." He grimaced.

"You're right. I apologise. And I am worried. You shouldn't be this bad. We need to bring you to hospital."

"I can drive us," he said.

"I'll do it, but I don't know the roads. You'll have to guide me."

"I'd rather stay here…not that I don't trust your driving skills," he said, trying not to laugh through the pain.

"I'm going to ask your brother to drive us to the closest hospital."

"Okay. I'm not sure he'll be willing to, but you can try."

I called Jay and told him what was going on, and he agreed to come get us.

I was so relieved.

So we all went to St. George's hospital in Kogarah, about fifteen minutes away. It was my first time in an Australian hospital. I spent the night by his side, waiting for the doctors to reduce his pain. He seemed embarrassed but happy to have me standing by him. They'd given him some painkillers, and we were waiting for the doctor.

I bought him some Cadbury chocolates from the vending machine and offered them to him, but he said he wasn't hungry.

"The doctors may not see me for a while," he said. "You don't have to stay."

"I want to. I don't have anything better to do, except sleep, of course. Unless I'm making you feel uncomfortable." I was tired, but I wanted to be there for him. He would have done the same for me.

"Exactly. You could sleep. You work tomorrow, and you're going to be exhausted."

"That's okay. I'm fine. Anyway, it shouldn't be much longer now. It's been more than an hour. I'm sure the doctor will come back soon."

Ten minutes later, the doctor examined him and recommended surgery to eradicate the problem once and for all. Justin needed to spend the night in observation and said he'd ask his brother to drive me home. At this point, I'd only be getting a couple of hours of sleep before I had to get up and go to work.

He said, "Thank you for caring for me like you did, tonight. I really appreciate it."

"That's normal," I said. "You're my boyfriend, right?"

"Many wouldn't have. Nobody has ever done that for me."

"Well, I'm special, so I did," I said and kissed him.

His brother drove me home, and we had a quick chat in the car. I found out he was single but had three kids from a previous relationship. They were now in foster care, because he had a conflicted relationship with his ex. He seemed okay with it, but I felt bad, as I couldn't imagine not being with my children if I had them some day.

Justin had his surgery, and by the next weekend, we were watching movies together, loved up on his couch. He was still in bad shape and couldn't work for a month. It was weird living a normal life with him, not visiting as a backpacker or a tourist anymore, but a permanent resident like everyone else. Justin seemed pleased that I stayed by his side, taking care of him. I thought it was the right thing to do. I missed him during the week, so I was happy to be with him after work and spend my time in his arms.

Justin made an effort the next Monday and picked me up after my shift at the café. We had a romantic walk through the botanical garden and enjoyed the sunset on the waterfront at the Rocks. It was a revealing time, as he couldn't work, so it was my turn to finance all our date nights. I even helped him by paying his rent, as his own mum didn't seem willing to help him out. It reminded me of Francois and how I used to help him, but I knew Justin was far more honest and humble. I just hoped I wasn't making a mistake.

By Thursday, April 14, 2011, after two months together, Justin was all healed. He came to the pub and stayed there with his mates until I finished. Then we went to the Toxheys Pub, further up on Glebe Point Road. We ordered a beer at the bar and sat outside in the smoking area. I was happy to finally relax after work.

I said, "I'm glad you don't smoke weed anymore. I know it was a lot for you, but I really appreciate that you quit for me. It's just a source of conflict, really."

I'd smoked when I was younger, and it was hard for me to give up, so I was surprised by how easy it had been for Justin.

"It's just a matter of willpower," he said. "Usually once I make a decision, I never go back on it. I knew you wouldn't stay with me otherwise, and I'd rather be with you."

"Thank you," I said. "I really want this relationship to work out. I mean, you're special to me, and I don't want anything to ruin what we have. But to be honest, I don't like that you still get weed for your mates. You quit, so you shouldn't be near any temptation."

"You don't trust me?"

"Of course I do."

"Well obviously not," he said, getting upset.

"Don't get mad. I didn't want you taking it the wrong way."

"Well, how do you want me to take that?"

"I just don't think it's a good idea, that's all. Why would you do that? It's their problem, so they can deal with it."

"I know the guy, that's all," he said. "I quit for you, so what more do you want from me?"

"I'd feel better if you stopped."

"You should just trust me."

"How could I trust that you're not smoking when you're not with me?"

"Because…"

"Why? Tell me," I said, pushing him.

"Because…I love you." He said these words meaningfully but like he wanted to shut me up at the same time. Great success.

"What?" I was shocked.

"I love you. That's why you should trust me. I would do anything for you."

His words comforted me. "Oh, really? Well, I love you too, Justin," I said, smiling now.

And I did trust him. For the past week, I'd been desperate to hear these words. I was happy. We were happy. All of a sudden, there was only the two of us in the courtyard, staring at each other with watery eyes and a big smile on our faces. It was like both of us needed to hear these words, and we felt even closer after sealing the love deal. We spent a lovely rest of the evening, closer than ever.

The following weekends we visited around to Parramatta markets, Balmain, Balmoral beach where we had a little dance in the garden kiosk, Shoulder Bay, and George Head. We loved spending time together, with him showing off his beautiful city. I'd never had that much fun or so many romantic walks.

Also, we were awkwardly followed by brides and grooms everywhere we went. It was probably because these romantic and beautiful places were also chosen by the newlyweds for their wedding pictures. Every time we met up, there they were. It was like a sign.

So early on, we started talking about how important marriage was for us. We both wanted the same thing in a relationship and agreed this one was serious. Also, we wanted to marry our soul mate for the forever commitment of love, because marriage was sacred, and divorce wasn't an option. The old couple from the Blue Mountains was our model of happiness. I was glad to have found someone who shared my values and thoughts about true love and marriage. He also wanted two children, just like I did.

Soon, it was Easter, and Justin brought me to the Sydney Royal Easter Show. I'd never seen anything like this. It was like a mixture of the Paris International Agricultural Show, the International Home Show in Nice, and a giant Luna Park, with trophies and all sorts of brand promotion in between. A massive field was covered with stalls and animals, rides and show bags, and all sorts of food. There was a giant arena with horses and old-school cowboy performances.

We had a wonderful time. It was an amazing surprise, and I felt like a little girl as I kept looking around everywhere, amazed by every detail. We enjoyed all the craziest rides and bought all those stupid pictures they sell you for a fortune. I'd seen a cute purple teddy bear, and Justin decided to win it for me. What a mistake. He nearly spent fifty bucks on this strong man hammer thing and didn't win it. I had to beg the guy and negotiate another ten bucks, but we got it.

He brought me back to my place, where we spent a long time kissing and talking at the front door. Then as I was walking back upstairs to my room, I opened the staircase window and accidentally dropped the teddy bear outside, where he fell over the neighbour's fence. I couldn't believe it. After Justin had spent so much effort trying to get the bloody bear. I had to get it back. I went straight to the neighbours and tried all the three bells of the intercom, but there was no answer. I panicked. I loved this bear, and it was my gentleman's first present to me, not counting all the roses.

I went back to my home and got a chair from the kitchen. Then I jumped on it and climbed the fence and into my neighbour's yard. I was scared, because this was so illegal. But Teddy was there, luckily not too wet, even after the bit of rain we'd had. To get back, I climbed on top of a bin before scaling the rest of the fence and jumping back into my side of the yard. Wow, that was something. Then I went upstairs, avoiding the dangerous window, and got ready for a good night's sleep.

But first, I had to call Justin to tell him about the crazy events, and we laughed. It was such a good day.

Easter was a long five-day weekend, which provided a good opportunity for Justin and I to spend more time together and also for him to introduce me to the rest of his family. On Easter Sunday, we drove to his uncle's house in Wollongong for their traditional family lunch. I met his mum, as well as her four brothers, Gino, Tony, Lino, and Pas, and their families. Jay was also there. I thought they were nice and chatted with all of them. They were nearly trying to marry us off already. Justin had never introduced them to anyone before, so I felt special and flattered once again.

Later, as Justin drove me through the city, we stopped at the lighthouse and admired the coastal beaches. He talked about his childhood there and decided to drive me around to show me his school and childhood neighbourhood. Between the suburb of housing and commissions he used to live in, his troubled past, and his complicated family, I should have run. But I loved him so much already, I stayed. He'd gone through a lot and created a better life for himself. He'd left everything behind and started over in Sydney, just like I had. He was such a great guy, and he didn't choose his childhood. Nobody does. That was what made him the amazing man I loved. He was so different from anyone I'd met before. He was special, and we had so much in common. We were from two different and faraway worlds, and we'd finally found each other, after so many years apart.

Once at my place, we got together with some of my friends. I cooked two delicious pizzas from scratch and my favourite chocolate fondant. We spent the rest of the night in Newtown, drinking and celebrating Tani's departure. My last friend in Australia was about to leave, so I figured maybe it was time for me to make the move, too.

7

On the weekend, I decide it's time to enjoy life and live mindfully, so we visit the Sydney Aquarium with Jack and have some wonderful family time. I enjoy every second of it, each smile and laugh. After a lunch on Darling Harbour and a chocolate ice cream, my favourite, we bring Jack to the playground and have fun in the water. He loves the fountains and the slides and is so happy. We all are. Okay, cancer and dying are always at the back of my mind, giving me a solemn reminder to take mental pictures of every minute of the day, but you see things like never before. Your whole world is brighter, more detailed, deeper, and somehow happier. We probably won't go to France now, but Justin promised me that we will go to Uluru and maybe Tasmania, like I've always wanted to.

One thing is sure for now. I'm reconsidering my job. My time is so precious, I should do something that will have more impact on people's lives. I've also decided to write my diaries in English from now on, so my children can read them if I'm not around to tell them my story. I hope I will, though. I'm looking at the world the way I used to when I arrived in Australia, with eyes wide open and no plans for the future. I'm living in the moment and appreciating everything around me, feeling my heart pumping and my lungs expanding.

I think about Justin, and I hope our love story is strong enough to do miracles and save me, so we can stay together. I love him so much, even through the bad times and the arguing. He makes me happy. I love his smile and his sense of humour, and along with our children, he's the best thing that's ever happened to me. I remember how he left everything for me and his beautiful proposal.

It was the end of April 2011, and it was time for me to make the big decision. I was already six months into my Working Holiday visa, and it would expire in another six months. I wanted to stay in Australia. The only way to renew it for another year was to go picking for three months. It was part of my plan from the start, but now that Justin was in the equation, I didn't want to leave him for so long. So on the last Thursday of the month, he came home after my shift, and we sat at the kitchen table to have a talk.

I explained that my visa would expire at the end of October and that I'd have to go away to do some picking. This meant finding a farmer who could guarantee me the hours and would sign the paperwork for the Australian Department of Immigration.

"Okay," he said. "But it doesn't sound easy."

"Well, that's for sure. But I really want to stay here, especially since I've met you. I can't help feeling sad. I'll miss you so much."

"I'll miss you too, my angel," he said.

"It's the only chance I've got, but I'm so scared of being away from you." I burst into tears.

"You're going to be fine." He took me in his arms and comforted me.

"But what if you forget me? Or you find someone else? I don't want to lose you."

"I would never do that. I love you. I won't forget you. You're my angel. Life is so much better with you. Maybe you'll find somebody else. Look how beautiful you are," he said with a smile, his eyes shining with tears.

"I don't want to leave without you."

"What do you want me to do?"

"I don't know. I'm lost. I love you so much, but at the same time, I have to go, otherwise I won't be able to stay with you. It's been so good between us. I really want to give us a chance, but three months far away from you seems like forever."

"Then I'll come with you," he said.

"Really?" I was surprised but happy.

"Yes, really. I want to be with you, too, so why not?"

"But what about your work?"

"I'll have to find a job wherever you'll go. I don't think it will be too hard."

"Oh my God. That's fantastic. Oh, I love you. You're the best. I can't believe you're doing this for me." I was so excited.

After this comforting conversation, I advised both my jobs that my last day would be May thirteenth, and that was it. I spent the next two weeks trying to figure out which part of Australia was the best for picking and started packing my bags. I called Harvest Australia for some information, and it didn't look good. There was nothing in the West for the moment, and if there was any picking, there were so many backpackers, I'd probably arrive too late. Also, Queensland was just recovering from the summer flooding. I didn't want to bring Justin with me into a trap, even if he thought that an Aussie like him could find a job anywhere. I was hoping I could sort something out quickly.

My regular customers at the pub were aware of my departure, and they all offered to help me out. That's so Australian, and I loved it. After a few days, one of them gave me the details of a farmer, Michael, who was cultivating mandarins in a small town near Bundaberg in Queensland and could offer me a job picking. I just had to call him once I was there. Awesome. Bundaberg it was.

This big jump into the unknown scared me, because it was also a big step forward for this three-month-old relationship. Justin and I had decided we would probably live together after the three months were over, as he would be replaced by another roommate, and I wouldn't have a place, either. Everything seemed to be going so fast, my head was spinning.

My disastrous past love stories didn't help my state of mind, and I started to have doubts. Justin was about to give most of his stuff to his best mate, Matt, and try to sell the rest to get some cash, as I'd been the one paying for everything since his surgery. Still, he was leaving everything behind to follow me on this crazy adventure, with nothing for sure once we got there. I was just hoping we wouldn't break up because we wanted to move too fast. All I wanted was a great trip together and that we'd both find a job, so we could come back to Sydney happier than ever.

We left, taking only Justin's bag of clothes and my luggage. We'd both quit our jobs and took to the road together for our big adventure, leaving our past behind, ready for the next chapter of our life together. I couldn't believe he'd left everything behind for me. Nobody had ever done that for me before. But the pressure was on. I couldn't screw it up. I was really hoping that Michael the farmer could help out. I needed it.

We spent our first week travelling across New South Wales and Queensland and sleeping in caravan parks in the small tent we'd purchased for the occasion. I loved camping, but Justin wasn't a fan, really. He kept saying, "I haven't worked my arse off all year just to rough it while on holidays." But I made it my mission to convince him it was great. On our way to Queensland, we stopped by Hat Head, Trial Bay

Gaol (an old jail), and then we travelled along the coastal beaches: South West Rock, Macksville, Coffs Harbour, and the Big Banana. I thought it was so funny that in Australia, they have all these *big* things. The big mango was in Bowen, regularly stolen for some reason. There was also the big pineapple, the big prawn, and the big potato…you name it. We tried to experience as many "big" things as possible.

We had a great time in a nice holiday park in Corindi, and I took some beautiful pictures of the sun rising on the ocean. Life was easy. It was the first time we'd spent that much time together and was our first holidays. Justin always listened to a classic rock radio station in the car, and I could now recognise some of the traditional Australian hits. It was like I was going back in time, between the old music, the camping, and the way Australians lived outside the big cities. It was so different from home.

Then we went through Grafton, Woodburn, Ballina, Murwillumbah, and the beautiful Natural Bridge National Park. It was lucky we had my *Lonely Planet* book, so we didn't miss the beauty of this park. It was mid-afternoon when we arrived there, and we decided to go for a romantic walk. We discovered a majestic waterfall in a cave full of glow worms. It was like the Milky Way was on the rock ceiling of the cave surrounding it. As it started getting darker outside, we walked back to the car through the dense rainforest, following the glow worms, now everywhere along the footpath. That was the most magical moment I'd ever witnessed. We were both amazed by the surreal surroundings offered to our mesmerised eyes. Then we drove off to find a camping spot in Burleigh Heads, on the Gold Coast.

The next morning, we got coffee from a French café before having a walk on the beautiful beach of Surfers Paradise. It was so nice to be together, discovering all these beautiful views of Australia by Justin's side. He could now see it all through my eyes, too. Everything from the shops, architecture, habits, and pubs, to the people, fashion, music, and even the brands and products, were so different. Not to mention the deadly spiders and snakes.

We left again to go across Brisbane and had lunch in Caboolture. Then we headed north to Noosa. On the way, we started arguing, because we hadn't found a place to stay yet, and it was getting late. Caravan parks were closing soon, and we were tired. Justin could be so stubborn sometimes, and he gave me the silent treatment instead of trying to resolve the issue.

I hated us being on bad terms, so when I realised the Surfer League Club was next to the Noosa River Caravan Park, where we wound up staying, I told Justin we should go for a drink and try to relax instead of butting heads. Before entering the club for karaoke night, I asked him for a smile and a hug to bury the hatchet, which he agreed to, and we had so much fun singing our song "Throw Your Arms Around Me." I was terrible but tried again with a Pink song, and we finished our night singing "With or Without You" by U2, which was one of my favourite songs. Justin hated karaoke, but he sang for crazy me. I didn't care, as I had no shame being a terrible singer and enjoyed the night laughing with my love.

After a few drinks, we were a bit tipsy, and we walked along the beach to get back to our little tent. Somehow, we got to talking about each other's faults. But instead of pulling us apart, it brought us closer. He told me that I questioned things too much, and I said he complained too much for my liking. But being on the road wasn't easy, especially when I was paying for everything, he was the one driving all the time, and we didn't speak the same language. It was hard enough for a man and a woman of the same mother tongue to understand each other, so you can imagine how bad it could get at times when the Martian and the Venusian don't speak the same language. But love arranges everything, and we didn't want to split. We agreed that understanding each other was also part of the love story.

I decided to help with the driving, which wasn't easy, considering I was on the wrong side of the road, and everything was opposite to what I was used to back home. I was happy when we left Noosa and its hundred roundabouts. His car, a little black Daihatsu Sherade, pimped with an imported Japanese engine, started having some issues, and we had to get it checked by the nearest mechanic in Gympie, a small town in the middle of nowhere.

We left the car at the garage, and while the guys were checking it out, we went to the local pub at the Freeman Hotel. I noticed that in Australia, even in the smallest cities with only one road, there was always a pub. The heart of the community, I guessed. Justin and I put our two dollars in the slot machine, and we'd made the better of sixty dollars when we left after a couple of beers.

Back at the garage, the mechanics told us that the car had nothing wrong with it. They just added a bit more water and cleaned up the spark plugs. Justin insisted on giving them a ten dollar note each for their help, and we were back on the road. I couldn't help but think how nice he was, even with people he didn't know. He was always so generous and positive about everything. I learned from him what it means to be really generous, without thinking of what you could get in return. Pure and genuine honesty and generosity. He believed that good karma was better than money, and he was definitely right.

We went through Maryborough and its classic old Queenslanders, and reached Hervey Bay by evening. We stopped at a tourist park on the beach for the night and had a lovely walk on the pontoon, watching the fishermen as the sun set in beautiful orange and pink colours, melting into the ocean. After a good night's sleep, we had a coffee on the beach and discovered the Marina and Shelly Beach before heading to our final destination, Bundaberg.

It was Justin's thirty-third birthday, and I wanted to celebrate it properly. We found a little cabin for the night, so he could be more comfortable sleeping in a proper bed rather than a tent. We had a couple of beers at the local pub, which were nearly half the price of what it cost in Sydney, and bought a couple of steaks, some veggies, and his favourite chocolate ice cream, so I could cook a nice birthday dinner. It was a nice change from the backpacker Chinese noodles rule. I offered him some Quicksilver clothes I'd purchased for the occasion back in Sydney and showed him how we wore lingerie in my country. We had a great night.

The next morning, we went for a walk in Bargara, had some fried chicken thighs we bought in a local shop, and spent the day on the beach, taking pictures and playing, until we once again watched the beautiful sunset. Then we went back to the cabin and organised an appointment over the phone for 8.30 a.m. with Michael, the farmer.

The next morning, we were on the road to the farm. It was close to Gin Gin, but we nearly got lost trying to get there and were anxious we would run out of fuel before finding the farm. Justin showed me how much he could swear, which I wasn't used to, and Michael wasn't in the walls when we got there twenty minutes after our appointment time. I talked to Mary-Ann, the manager, and she confirmed that there would probably be some work for us during the week and would get back to me the next morning.

We drove around to find a caravan park to stay overnight. There was no way I was sleeping in the scary Gin Gin Caravan Park. Not only wasn't I sure we could get out of there due to all the mud, but there were lots of boxes of wine around, and it was still morning. It looked like people lived there full time, doing nothing but drinking and swearing. We asked for a refund at reception and left as quickly as possible. After driving farther out, we found a beautiful caravan park on Lake Monduran. We were the only customers and camped on a green landscape, in the middle of a massive park, in communion with the wild. It was quiet, beautiful, and so relaxing, especially compared to the crazy place we'd just left.

Two days later, we hadn't heard from Mary-Ann or Michael. I started to panic and called Harvest Jobs, the government phone line for picking. They advised me to go through a backpacker hostel, as they were the ones providing picking jobs in the area. The only problem was that we had to pay nearly two hundred dollars a week each to sleep with ten other backpackers. Justin didn't want to stay in a hostel or do any picking, because he was Australian and could earn his living better than that. Also, he didn't understand why we had to live that way when we could rent a full house for ourselves for less money.

As a backpacker, I understood. Real estate agents wouldn't lease anything to us, and farmers were aware we had to do picking to renew our visas, so they exploited us. I didn't know what to do. I was a backpacker, but he wasn't. I had to renew my visa, and he didn't. I had to do some picking, while he could get his good job back. I understood the hostel concept, even if they were screwing backpackers in need by abusing the system. We were from two different worlds, and our love story was being threatened by a stupid visa.

Justin and I went to the local pub in Bundaberg to try and figure out what to do.

"So, what options are available for you to be able to stay in Australia with me?" he asked.

"Well, after working for three months, I'll be able to stay for another year and only be able to work six months at a time for the same employer, and probably only in hospitality, because no company would hire a backpacker to do marketing, especially for such a short time. Then I'd have to go back home, as I can't stay more than two years, unless we get a de facto partner visa."

"Well, one thing's for sure," he said. "I'm not staying here without a job, and there's no way I'll live in a hostel full of backpackers."

"There's still the option of you coming home with me," I said with a smile.

"Hmm, I'll pass. I love my country and you're the one who came here. Besides, I don't speak French."

"You're right," I said. "I left my country for a reason."

"What about the de facto visa. Can't we do that?"

"Well, the problem is that you have to prove you've been together a year, and it's only been three months. I can't stay for more than a year in the country. I would be an illegal immigrant.

"Stupid rules." He paused for a moment then said, "Well, maybe we should think about getting married, then."

I was startled by his suggestion, but happily so. "You know how I feel about marriage. It's not something I take lightly. If I marry you, it's because you're my soul mate, and not for a visa. And it's only been three months. I love you, but I don't want to rush into anything. Anyway, it's getting late. We should get back before dark."

On the way back to the park, we knew two things for sure: there was no way I'd stay there picking without him, and we wouldn't spend even a day apart. When we got back, we walked to Lake Monduran and were watching the eagles fly, still trying to find a solution.

"So you're saying that without picking, there's no way to renew your visa?" Justin was having a hard time understanding the immigration laws.

"Yes, pretty much. I could do construction, too," I said with half a smile. "Just thinking of you going back to Sydney without me, breaks my heart."

"I know, but I can't find a job here. It's crazy. I asked everywhere in the city, but they're not looking for labourers. I can't believe it. I've never had trouble getting a job before." He was actually upset, unused to being told he wasn't needed.

"I'm sorry I made you come all this way here. You left everything for me, and now we both end up with nothing. I guess once I find a job picking, I could live out of a backpack for the next three months, but I can't picture myself being here without you."

"I know," he said. "Maybe we should just go back to Sydney. I could get my old job back and put some money aside, so I could propose later, and we could get married before your visa expires."

"Are you proposing to me?"

"Look, with a Working Holiday visa, you can't find the job you really want anyway, and I really think you're the one for me. We could get married, so I could keep you here forever. I don't take marriage lightly, either. I never really thought I'd get married, because I couldn't have imagined meeting someone like you, especially a French girl." He laughed.

I said, "I love you, but you know if I get married, it's forever. I want to spend the rest of my life with you."

"I've never been more serious. I love you," he said and kissed me.

"I love you too, Justin, but I need to think about it. I don't want to rush anything."

"Take your time," he said. "It's up to you. We'll do whatever you want."

And that's how Justin proposed, watching the sunset on the beautiful Lake Monduran. Again, he showed me how different he was compared to the other men from my past. He would do anything for me. He wanted to stay by my side forever and definitely wanted to keep me in his wonderful country. I'd fallen in love with him and his country, but not his family. That was the only thing that stopped me from saying yes straight away that night.

The next morning, Justin and I didn't talk about it. I was anxious. I wrote in my diary, took pictures, sunbathed…all without saying a word. I had to choose what I wanted to do, and it was driving me crazy. I wondered if I would be able to stay here for him, so far away from my family, without anything being sure.

We had no money except for the five thousand dollars I'd saved, and we had no work. He could probably get his job back, as we'd only been gone ten days. I knew it wouldn't take me long to find one, either, even if it wasn't in marketing. Then, if I wasn't able to stay, I would have to leave in a few months. I felt sad thinking about not being with him anymore and going back to my old depressing life, leaving the happy one behind. I couldn't go backward. There was no way I would let this happen.

We left Lake Monduran the next day, our decision made that we would go back to Sydney. He called his mum who said we could take the bedroom downstairs at their place for thirty dollars rent a week. It took us only two days to drive back to the big city, and when we went to his best mate to get all his stuff back, Matt told him that it was his now. He didn't want to give Justin anything back. I couldn't believe that. Justin had really lost everything with my stupid trip. Back at his old place, his brother had taken his old bedroom, so we didn't even have a bed to sleep on. I broke down in tears, thinking that it was my fault, I felt awful. We even asked the police for help, but they said that because Justin gave his stuff to his mate, it was his word against Matt's, and they couldn't do anything. I was outraged.

From that day on, Justin didn't have friends anymore. "They always let you down" was his motto. We were lucky to have our camping air bed to sleep on. We lived in a bedroom with no furniture, and we had to take the outside stairs to access the rest of the house where his mum and brother were living.

On top of that, I realised how weird his family was. I knew from before that they weren't all that close, which was different from what I was used to in so many ways. For example, back home, we all ate together and chatted around the dining table, sharing conversations and feelings. Justin's family ate separately, one in each bedroom, with his mum in the lounge room. She also stuck tags everywhere around the house, reminders of what we could and couldn't do, instead of just telling us.

On top of the heavy tension at home, I was now two hours away by train from the city and found it difficult to find a job in the area, even if Justin was driving me everywhere for job interviews whenever possible.

8

It's Wednesday, and I have an appointment with my oncologist, who's apparently one of the best, if not *the* best, in Australia for melanoma. We're about to leave home when I fall into tears thinking it could be the end and that I may not be here for my newborn, my son, and my husband. I also get upset with Justin, because he's letting me cry alone.

"Can you come and comfort me, please? I'm so sad," I say, sobbing.

"Why are you crying? I'm sorry we haven't left yet. I'm ready now." He looks at me, seemingly baffled by my emotions.

"I'm not crying for that," I snap.

"What are you crying for, then?"

"Because I'm so scared of dying. I want to see my babies grow up. I want to be there for you…"

"I'm scared, too. Oh, darling," he says and takes me into his arms as he also falls into tears.

"Are you?" I ask surprised.

"Of course."

"Why?"

"If something happens to you, I don't know what I'll say to our kids. How am I going to tell them mummy isn't here anymore? That she's gone forever…" He's struggling to articulate. "What would I do without you? I'm lost without you. I won't be able to do anything without you." By now he's completely sobbing.

"I'm so sorry, love. I'm sorry this is happening to us."

"You don't have a choice. You have to survive. You have to live. You can't leave me. I'm nothing without you, I need you," he replies, wiping his tears.

"I promise I'll try my best, but I can't guarantee anything. I don't want to let you down. I feel awful doing this to you and the kids."

We cry for a while in each other's arms, until we realise it's late, and we have to go. We dry our tears, swallow our sobs, and leave home. It's by far the hardest and saddest conversation I've ever had and one of the most painful moments of my entire life. But the truth is that this surreal situation is indeed sad. All the doctors, all our friends, have told us what a tragedy it is to be pregnant and have cancer. How sad that what should be one of the happiest moments for our family, is threatened by the fact that I may not last long enough to see my babies grow up.

If some director wanted to make a movie out of this, it would probably be a flop, because people would think the situation was a bit intense and way too over the top to be realistic. But it is real. And Justin is right, I have no choice in the matter. I have to fight this with all my strength and survive. I can't let them down. I hope I'll survive and never have cancer anymore, ever again. I want to live happily forever, with my little family.

I haven't told anyone else about what's going on. Even Justin's family is unaware of the situation. I just want to survive and pretend nothing's happened and have it gone as fast as it came. I hope by some miracle that if it began with my pregnancy, it will go away after the delivery.

Once I'm with the oncologist, she gives me the option of two different clinical trials if I'm at stage III. Like any cancer, the determination of the gene mutation in the cancerous cells is crucial in finding an appropriate treatment. I have a BRAF mutation, like forty per cent of people with melanoma do, so I can participate in a clinical trial that would allow me to take a combination of two drugs, a therapy that targets the cancerous cells, already approved for stage IV melanoma. In ninety percent of cases, it helps to significantly shrink the tumours, so if I decide to take this trial, the surgery to remove the lymph nodes would be postponed for at least three months. The surgery would also be easier, because the tumours would be smaller. Then I'd continue taking these drugs for another nine months.

The other clinical trial is randomised. I would have surgery and then I would either be in a placebo group, so I'd have no treatment, or in a group receiving immunotherapy. Apparently, immunotherapy boosts your own immune system to fight the cancer cells, limiting the reoccurrence. She gives me all the paperwork to read and study, but beforehand, I have to do a PET scan to make sure I'm in stage III. If I'm in stage IV, it's another story.

Once back at home, I discuss my options with Justin. All these pages of medical trials are difficult to understand, even if my oncologist did pretty well explaining most of the medical jargon to us. We just want to be sure I make the right decision. After all, my life is on the line.

The reality is that I'm terrified. I'm scared, because I don't know how long I have left. Justin doesn't want to know my prognosis and convinces me not to ask my oncologist about it. But knowing how long I could last without treatment wouldn't be helpful anyway, because I'm going to do a clinical trial, and there aren't any statistics available yet for the results. I hope I'm only in stage III, so I have a better chance at surviving this. Seeing my kids go to school and get married would be fantastic. I'm so scared and confused right now. I came to Australia, because it was my dream. It's only been five years. Now that I have everything I ever wanted, I may lose it all.

Back in Sydney, I was hopeless, feeling down, in a position even worse than ever before. Justin and I were more in love than ever. It was my only saving grace. He said that if we had to get married to stay together, it would be rushing things a bit, but he would do it, because he really thought I was The One, the love of his life. It would be easier once I became a permanent resident, but I didn't want people thinking we were getting married for a visa. I knew how it was. I'd been the first one to point a finger at my sister's first husband, an illegal immigrant in France, who got papers as soon as he married Laetitia and later treated her like crap.

I loved Justin, and if I married him, I'd do it because I really thought he was the best man I'd ever met. He was affectionate, funny, generous, genuine, and hardworking. And on top of it all, he was a real gentleman. We watched movies together at night, curled up in the couch. He prepared my coffee every morning, and the sex had never been so good.

Okay, money was missing from the equation, but he worked hard and knew how to prioritise. The most important thing was that we were in love, and we shared the same values. It was hard for me to lose my independence, as he was now the only one working. Also, I was in the middle of his divided family and not so sure about what the future held. I hated not being in control and facing uncertainty. It made me feel lost and vulnerable. But one thing was for sure: I was learning to let go and stay positive. I printed out a bunch of resumes, determined to find a job in marketing. In life, nothing is easy. I just had to deal with it, like I always had.

Thinking of marriage was scary and exciting at the same time. But the signs had been there, with all the newlyweds following us on our romantic dates. We were talking about it more and more, and even figured out that we'd need a babysitter for our kids—a boy and a girl, we agreed—because his family wouldn't be helpful.

My parents and sister were supportive, though Laetitia was a bit reluctant at first, because of her marriage experience. And even if we got married in Australia, we could give them another beautiful wedding back home, at the church. They didn't know Justin, but after all the guys I'd been with, my dad was convinced that if I'd picked this one to be my husband, he would be The One for sure. The most important thing was that we loved each other. Nothing else mattered.

In mid-June, I got a sales job working for a gold buyer in shopping centres. It was weird, boring, and definitely time-consuming, as I had to go to shopping centres around the city by train. But it was a job. Things couldn't have been better between Justin and me, and we were about to move into a better flat. His mum continued to stress me out, always whinging about everything and asking Justin for the money he owed her for the rent and all the bills she'd paid for him after his surgery. I paid her back with my savings and was glad to leave her house. I didn't think she liked me much. She was against this wedding, thinking it was too early. And she also didn't understand the visa situation, probably thinking I was using her son. Anyway, we were about to be on our own, living the couple's life and preparing for our wedding.

After two weeks, I quit my job. The travel was driving me insane, and I barely had the time to see Justin, because I worked on weekends, too. It was better for me to find a job in marketing, and I would take the time I needed to find one. Meanwhile, I was playing the perfect housewife, cooking meals, cleaning, washing clothes, and exercising.

But I was still desperate to find an office job. Employers were reluctant to give me one, because of my visa situation. I couldn't work more than six months for the same boss, and that was definitely a deal breaker. It was nice of Justin to take care of us, without questioning it. He didn't care. He just wanted me happy. He knew how to make me feel better when I was down, and even though we'd settled into a routine, we were falling deeper in love every day.

He wanted to offer me a beautiful engagement ring and was trying hard to save money. We began thinking of how our life would be once we were married. We wanted to have kids and a house, and even imagined building one from scratch. There would be big windows, lots of them, and a large bathroom, so we could still have our showers together. We'd have one bedroom for our son and another for our daughter, as well as a pool, a large lounge room, a home cinema, and a massive screen to watch movies, with recliners and drink holders. It was nice to dream out loud together, laughing about it, because we were still sleeping on our camping air bed.

By the end of August, I became a marketing executive for a company that sold conferences and workshops to professionals. I was doing a lot of social media promotion, emailing, and definitely improving my English and digital skills. I worked hard, but I was happy to finally have a job in my field of study. They accepted my application, because I was engaged. Justin was proud of me, and we were now living the way a married couple should. I had the routine I thought I'd never wanted: work, train, sleep…and I loved it. Justin had started helping me with the chores, as I couldn't do them all by myself anymore. I'd leave home early and come back late. The commute to and from my work in St. Leonards took three hours.

Also, I was preparing everything for the wedding. I found my custom-made dress for under two hundred dollars on a Chinese website that took only a month to make and bought a great pair of shoes. Then I booked the date with the Registry of Birth, Deaths, and Marriages in Parramatta, as we didn't have the time or the money to find a celebrant and get married on the beach. We chose the first of October for our wedding day. It was Labour Day, and we were pleased that we'd have a long weekend every year to celebrate our anniversary.

We also bought the rings. Justin chose a bridal set for me, and I picked a nice white gold wedding band for him. I also planned a pamper day for myself the day before the wedding, with a full body massage and a mani-pedi. I wished I could have done that with my sister, but unfortunately, she wouldn't be there. I'd have to get married without my family. Justin told me we only needed two witnesses, but I wanted to celebrate that day, and I thought it would be nice to have his family with us. After all, they would be mine soon as well, and we would go to France to get married later when we could afford it.

I was so happy but scared at the same time, because it was the beginning of a new life in Australia, forever far away from my affectionate family. His was absent and didn't really care for us, except maybe his dad and his girlfriend. I had trouble picturing never seeing mine again…not the way I used to, anyway. But I loved Justin, and I reminded myself why I left France, which was to create my own life. Luckily, I did. I'd found The One. Even if it meant I had to live without my family, I would create my own here. It would be tough for me, but it would be better for my kids. I knew I was doing the right thing, but I couldn't help thinking about my parents. Dad never told me he'd had a MALT lymphoma, a cancer he'd been diagnosed with in January that they discovered when he'd had stomach surgery for an ulcer, which he also hadn't told me about.

Mum was still coping with her health, too. My twin had just had her first baby, a little girl named Emy, and my grandma was losing her mind and moved into a nursing home. I thought they needed me, and I missed them, lots! My friends, too. All my backpacking buddies were gone, having returned to their country. I was the last woman standing! I may not have had many friends, but they were still there for me, despite the distance. It was a big move, and I started to get cold feet!

I announced the wedding by email and Facebook, and everyone was really happy for me, for us, even if they didn't know Justin. He told his family the same way but didn't get any reply. That's when we decided not do much after the ceremony. So I arranged to just open a tab where we met, at the AB Hotel, in the nice function room upstairs that had an eight-metre fish tank bar. We would have some drinks to welcome everyone, and that would be enough. We were broke anyway, and the most important thing was to get married and start our life together. Justin was already thinking of having kids with me.

A week before the wedding, Justin officially proposed. Better late than never. Besides the original "proposal", he'd also asked me while we were playing Fable III, a video game on Play Station. Even though I'd never played video games, he'd insisted, and I came to understand why, when he used his knight character to propose to my lady character. We even had the wedding at the castle, followed by the honeymoon night.

Then he'd proposed at the Royal National Park, while we were in a rowboat, and we nearly went overboard when he tried to get down one knee. The next time was at home, when we were about to watch a movie, and he'd proposed with a box containing a Magnum Ego ice cream. So, yes, he'd proposed many times, but never with my engagement ring, which had arrived only ten days before the wedding.

He surprised me by inviting me to a great seafood restaurant and booked a table with a view of the Opera House and the Sydney Harbour Bridge. It was beautiful, and our seafood platter was scrumptious. Before the dessert, he went down one knee with the box opened on a beautiful diamond ring, and proposed. I'd waited so long for that moment.

He said, "Karine, you're so beautiful. Nothing is more important than you in my eyes. I don't think I could ever live without you. You're my everything. Would you marry me?"

I felt like I was in a movie. It was weird hearing "Would you marry me?" in English. I was ecstatic. They were the most beautiful words anyone had ever said to me. Of course, I said "Yes." I was happy and flattered. People were looking at us as I helped him stand back up for a tender kiss. It's definitely the best night I'd ever had up until that point.

On September 30, 2011, a day before our wedding, everything was ready: the shoes, the beautiful dress I'd ordered, and the rings. I was getting nervous, but deep down, I was ecstatic. After all the years of looking for The One, I was finally making my dream come true. My family wouldn't be present, and there wouldn't be any cake or photographer, but the most important thing was that Justin and I would celebrate our love. Nothing else mattered. I was glad I'd booked my pampering session, because I definitely needed to unwind, and the massage and mani-pedi brought me to a peaceful stage. Everything was ready, including me, for the blissful day.

I woke up at eight a.m. to an empty flat, as I'd told Justin to sleep at his dad's, in order to keep with the tradition of spending the night apart before the wedding. I was super excited, and I couldn't be happier. I took a quick shower and put on some makeup. I had an appointment with the hairdresser down our street, so he could do my hair for the big day and was about to leave, when the intercom rang. I wasn't expecting anyone this early in the morning. I opened the door, and to my surprise discovered a big bouquet. It was the first time in my life someone had delivered flowers to me.

They were from my parents. I nearly cried that they wouldn't be with me, but I was so thankful they were sending me some love. I called them straight away. With an eight-hour time difference, it was late at night there, but my dad answered and was glad to hear I'd received the flowers he'd ordered for me. I thanked him and Mum for this great surprise. I didn't have a bridal bouquet, so I asked for permission to create one, as it would keep them close to me. Once they agreed, I took the flowers out of the foam, placed them in a round bouquet, and attached the lot with the ribbons of all the bouquets Justin had offered me so far and that I'd kept for the memories. It was beautiful, and I had a smile of satisfaction looking at my creation.

The sun was out, and the hairdresser did a great job with my hair, placing it in a braided bun, surrounded by a crown of pearls made of the same necklace I was wearing. I added some pearl earrings and a bracelet. I just had to put on my dress, and I was ready to go.

When I got back from the hairdresser, Belinda, Justin's dad's girlfriend, came with a bottle of bubbly, and we celebrated with a glass before I put on the gorgeous gown. I loved this dress. We put on some music, and with Belinda's enthusiasm, the bubbles, the lovely hairstyle, my gorgeous French manicure, and the flowers, I felt the perfume of happiness in the air. I really felt like a princess, with my sleeveless corset, tightened by a long ribbon at the back, embellished by pearls at the front. My waist was accented, as the tight top went down my hips to a beautiful asymmetrical gown made of lace and silk, and finished by a short train. I couldn't wait to be with my future husband.

Justin sent me a text message saying that after more than fifteen hours without me, he was lost already. It was so sweet. I put on a white fur shawl, fingerless white gloves, and my stilettos to finalise my look. I was just in time, as Justin's father, Stephen, arrived at the door to drive us to the Registry Office of Death, Birth, and Marriages. After telling me how stunning I looked, Stephen and Belinda helped me downstairs and into the car, and we arrived after a forty-five-minute drive.

I entered the building and found Justin's uncle, Gino, his wife. Shauna, and their two sons, his mum, Nina, and his brother, Jay, as well as Belinda's brother, Hamish…but there was no sign of Justin. After kissing and passing by everyone, I finally saw him. He was sitting at the back of the waiting room, so sexy in his black suit, with his black tie and a fresh haircut. He stood, kissed me quickly, and told me I was beautiful. We were excited, awkwardly shy, and a bit lost.

We waited for everyone to arrive for about fifteen minutes, which felt like forever. The sunny sky was slowly getting covered by clouds, but we still wanted to proceed. Then I chose the only Registry in Sydney with a garden, as I wanted to get married outside.

I was a bit disappointed when I realised that our guests would have to stand, and that they would unfold a plastic table covered with just a white tablecloth for us to sign the official papers. But nothing would take the smile from my face on our big day. It was nice to feel the fresh air and somehow be close to nature. The wedding was short but emotional for us.

After the celebrant made sure we were both free to get married, Justin and I held each other's hands, face to face, and exchanged our vows. My Justin was serious, and I could see in his eyes how important this moment was for him, too. He was so cute when he said "I do."

Then, it was my turn. My English was a bit lacking, with the emotions flooding through me and the smile clenching my jaw, but I managed to follow the celebrant's lead. My voice was weak, but my heart was bursting with love, and I knew my eyes were full of affection as I faced the man I'd spend my life with. I finally pronounced the words, "Yes, I do" with a huge smile. The exchange of the rings was a big moment, too. Very symbolic. Finally, we were given the go-ahead with, "I declare you husband and wife. You may now kiss the bride." We kissed passionately, followed by a long cuddle. His loving arms felt so comfortable and reassuring.

The whole time, it was like it was just the two of us and the celebrant, no one else. No witnesses, no family, just me and Justin, immersed in each other's eyes, face to face, hands in hands, wrapped in our loving bubble. So when the kiss happened, it was the same; two people crazy in love, smooching madly after a day apart and such a long wait. I felt so blessed. We'd never been happier, and we were now husband and wife.

Everything went so fast, like in the most beautiful dream. We signed the official paperwork, still shaking with emotions, and everybody congratulated us. Then we took some pictures and invited everyone to join us at the AB Hotel, where the function room awaited. His mum and Jay, his uncle Pas, and girlfriend, Luisa, couldn't stay, but the rest of our family and friends came over for some drinks.

When we arrived at the pub, my former bosses welcomed us with big applause, and the rest of the pub followed. Everyone there was congratulating us, and we enjoyed drinks and laughter in the upstairs function room for the rest of the day. For sure, when I'd started working at the pub back in December 2010, I hadn't known that one day I would meet my future husband there and later come to celebrate in my wedding dress, hand in hand with him.

Around eight p.m., we left the hotel to start our honeymoon at the Harbour View Hotel, in a beautiful suite on the thirteenth floor. That was Justin's surprise for me. I hadn't eaten all day, and with all the drinks I'd had, I was tipsy and needed some food. Justin had to stop me, otherwise I would have had takeaway pizza, while still wearing my wedding dress. What a day it was. We had so much fun. We were in love, and even if it was raining, it was all sunshine in our hearts.

The next morning, we were both hungover, and my darling husband went to grab us some coffee and a bacon and egg muffin for me. Nothing beats greasy food for hangovers. I called my parents to let them know how it went. It was only eight a.m., and my dad was surprised to receive my call, but happy to hear that I was now a married woman. I hung up when Justin came back with the yummy breakfast. We were so happy that morning, waking up for the first time as husband and wife.

Hamish came to pick us up around ten a.m. We had just enough time to get a shower and pack away all our stuff that was lying all over the floor.

Then we went home quickly to swap our bag of summer clothes for warmer ones, as the weather would be rainy up the coast. We left an hour later for Avoca Bay, where we spent our short honeymoon—three days of romance, love, and relaxation. We enjoyed a sumptuous suite with a spa bath, and we were welcomed with champagne and chocolate-coated strawberries.

Terrigal, the main city of the bay, was beautiful, and we appreciated doing nothing but relaxing, walking hand in hand along the beach, laughing, and kissing. We went to a French seafood restaurant and took lots of pictures. We were just living in the moment. It was too short, but it was so nice to be together. We hadn't had any holidays since our road trip, and this time, we were married.

After so many emotions, it was hard to go back to work, especially since I'd decided to quit smoking that day. Justin and I wanted babies, and there was no way I would fall pregnant while being a smoker.

I spent the rest of October finalising the three-hundred-page document required for my partner visa application and giving up three thousand dollars for it. My parents came for the Christmas holidays and met Justin for the first time. It was quite tough being on top of each other for three weeks, frenetically visiting a new place every day, which included Sydney CBD, Taronga Zoo, the Rocks markets, and the Queen Victoria Building, but I loved spending time with them. We played tourist guides, and Mum and Dad loved Australia.

They also appreciated Justin very much. It was the first time in my life that I felt like my parents really appreciated the man I'd chosen. Mum tried to communicate with hand signs and facial expressions. She didn't speak English but laughed at his jokes anyway. Dad helped him do the Christmas cake, and they argued over who would pay for our meals. We decorated the Christmas tree and enjoyed quality family time together. The week before Christmas, we visited Sydney, while Christmas day was spent at the beach. We then left for Cairns, the Great Barrier

Reef, Justin's dream destination, and Fitzroy Island the week after. It was our first proper holiday together and a sort of second honeymoon for us, especially in Fitzroy Island. I figured that the less there was to do, the better the holiday would be, since we couldn't do anything else but relax. We discovered the tropical weather, the beauty of secluded beaches, colourful fishes, and the magical reef.

After hard goodbyes to my tourist parents, we spent the weekend watching movies and spooning on the couch.

I had to leave my job before Christmas. Even though my partner visa had been granted, I still had to abide by the conditions of my working visa. So while I'd enjoyed my holidays, I'd also been thinking about looking for a new job as soon as we got back to Sydney.

In February, we moved to a bigger flat with two bedrooms, storage, and a garage. It was in Bexley, closer to the M5 motorway, and more central to Justin's work. I once again became a desperate housewife, but this time I enjoyed it a bit more. The flat wasn't renovated but was spacious, and I was glad to unpack the few boxes we had to make it our home.

The rent was cheap, so we could save money to buy a house later. Once my working conditions changed, and my partner visa was approved, I found a marketing executive position in a company five kilometres away. Patience always paid off. We couldn't be happier. We'd started out broke, but we were slowly achieving a better life, definitely stronger and happier together. My first work assignment was to go to the annual sales meeting the first week of June, in Fiji. I was over the moon. Life was finally smiling at me. What more could I ask for? Maybe a baby?

We were adjusting to our married life, to the role each of us had to play in our household and the daily routine. Even though we both worked hard, we still tried to have a couple of romantic weekends together visiting Jervis Bay with its beautiful white sand beaches, and Canberra to see Uncle Tony.

We also enjoyed renovating second-hand furniture found in council clean-ups and watching movies on the couch. Since we were both working, we could afford to live a bit more, and it was nice to feel like we were moving forward. As with any married couple, we had some tough times trying to find our way, but we were happy, and the arguments helped us understand each other better, compromise, and get closer. Though different, we complemented each other. The most important thing was that we shared the same vision for our future: a happy and close family.

In August, we were able to buy a bigger second-hand car that would accommodate a potential baby. Justin offered me the Harbour Bridge Climb for my thirty-first birthday and planned a road trip around New Zealand for our next Christmas holidays. We spent our first wedding anniversary in the beautiful Southern Highlands region and fell in love with it.

New Zealand was amazing. We were delighted by the geothermal park and its colourful grounds and rocks, where we soaked in the hot lakes, spreading smelly mud all over us. We celebrated Christmas in Rotorua with some barbecued ribs, drove along the dangerous roads of the South Island, saw lots of sheep, and the greenest landscapes.

We missed out on our helicopter flight because of the weather and struggled to find a caravan spot for New Year's Eve at Lake Wanaka. Thanks to Justin, I fought one of my biggest fears and bungee jumped in Queenstown at the Nevis Bungee, the highest jump in the southern hemisphere at one hundred and thirty-four metres. Another tick off my bucket list.

Then we ended in Harrow Town, a small village near Queenstown, where we had a great time at the local pub, meeting new people, and after the crazy bungee jump, went south to discover the wonderful Doubtful Sound and the Cadbury factory. We finished our trip in Christchurch, sadly unchanged since the 2010 earthquake. I twisted my ankle and fainted on our way to the airport, and was unable to walk for six weeks. We had an amazing time, even though Justin hadn't been too keen about doing a road trip in a caravan for three weeks, and we planned to make children our next adventure.

9

It's time. After spending the past two weeks organising the delivery of my second child, the day has come for me to leave home with my bag, my husband, and my son for a quick stay at St. George's hospital. I'm feeling anxious but prepared. After all, it's my third pregnancy. I already gave birth once, and despite the circumstances, everything went well. It's Sunday, October 25, 2015, at one o'clock in the afternoon when I arrive at the maternity ward, and I'm waiting for the obstetric team to show me my room. Then a friendly nurse calls my name.

"Yes, that's me," I answer with a bit of apprehension.

"So, you're here for an induction, is that right?"

"Yes."

"I'll show you to your room, and then we'll prep you. Did the obstetrician explain to you what's going to happen?

"Yes. I came last week to prepare everything for the birth and have my steroid injections. She said you'll monitor the baby and apply a gel to provoke the contractions."

"Right. The gel rarely works, but we'll try. And if it doesn't, we'll inject a hormone to start the labour. Are you okay?"

"I have to say, I'm a bit scared. You know, my first baby was very premature, and I'm afraid to have another one after all we've done to avoid it with the progesterone treatment."

"You're going to be fine. It's rare for the first injection to lead to labour. Mums usually need two of them before feeling contractions. I know this must be hard due to your circumstances, but you're in good hands"

They organised a room just for me, which is a nice touch, and Justin and Jack spend the next couple of hours with me before heading to their ward.

The nurse starts with the gel at four p.m. But after two hours, nothing has happened, so they give me the first injection of Prostaglandin. After six hours, still nothing, so at one a.m., I receive a second injection. Ten minutes later, the contractions start… and wow, are they painful. I don't recall my contractions for Jack being this bad. They're violent and close to one another.

At 1:30 a.m., I'm transferred to the delivery suite. Justin is by my side half an hour later. He'd been in Jack's room in the children's ward, which is on the same level as the maternity ward. It's comforting to have him here from the beginning this time.

They're giving me some gas, and even though it didn't do anything for me during Jack's birth, this time I feel like I'm flying. It's working, and I'm pumping on the machine like a maniac. Justin laughs, but I have to take it. The pain is unbearable, and I ask for an epidural. When the anaesthetist finally comes at 3:15 a.m., I have to decide against it. I've gone from three centimetres to six in half an hour, and they tell me that at this rhythm, the epidural won't kick in before the delivery. I'm also scared of the big needle, because I'd have to stay still while they perform the injection, even with the crazy pain and contractions, and I'm afraid it's going to be impossible.

But after twenty minutes, the pain is still intense, so I decide to go for it. I hope it will work fast enough and kick in before the birth. It's already painful enough. After the suffering I experienced pushing out tiny Jack, I don't feel like going through it with a nearly three-kilo baby. The morphine and gas aren't enough.

Another twenty minutes later, I'm sitting on the edge of my bed, trying to stay still, holding Justin's hand and praying it will be fine. I'm scared of doing this epidural while I have cancer. It's silly, but after all, who knows what the side effects could be? While enduring the pain of labour, I stay as still as possible for fifteen minutes, getting it out of my system through breathing and grunting. After the local anaesthesia comes the massive needle. Then a little while later, the drug kicks in, and I'm glad I've done it. What a relief. Okay, it would have been nice to pretend I was a warrior and give birth with no painkillers, but I wouldn't change a thing. I can feel the contractions but without the pain. I even get the chance to rest a bit and nearly fall asleep.

Around 4:30 a.m., Justin has to go put Jack to bed. He woke up when they came to get Justin, and he's been playing ever since.

At 6:30 a.m., I'm fully dilated, and the midwife nudges me to let me know we're proceeding with the delivery. They calmly tell me how to push with each contraction and breathe through them. I have to push three or four times, and everything is in the breathing. I don't have any pain, but I still feel what's happening, and it's an amazing experience. I don't have any stress and can peacefully focus on breathing and pushing, photographing every second into my memory. The only problem is that I can't feel my legs, so when one of them falls to one side, they have to move it for me.

I'm a bit disappointed that Justin doesn't want to film the delivery, so halfway through, they show me what's happening with a small mirror. I can see the hair on my baby's head coming out. They even tell me I can touch it. So beautiful.

At 7:56 a.m., I give birth. Justin has tears in his eyes, and again, when they place our baby on my bare chest, he says, "Look, it's a girl." I can't believe it's real. All that time, I was right—we were right. We knew it would be a beautiful baby girl, and here she is, covered in vernix and so calm. The entire thing was such a breeze. She's a miracle. I got what I wanted; my gorgeous girl. We call her Elyze, the only name Justin and I had agreed upon. A beautiful name for our beautiful daughter.

I ask them not to cut the cord straight away, so they wait nearly fifteen minutes before asking Justin to do it. Elyze is so peaceful, resting on my chest, sleeping, like nothing happened, like she's still inside me. She stays there for another two and half hours. I'm so happy to be able to keep her against me.

Then they weigh her and give her vitamin K and the hepatitis C vaccine. She weighs 2.86 kilograms, measures fifty centimetres, and was born at thirty-six weeks and three days, as expected. I'm so glad she's healthy, needs neither oxygen nor help to breathe, and doesn't have to go to the NICU. I can keep her with me. After about forty minutes, she even starts breastfeeding. I realise how much I missed out on with Jack's birth. I wish I could have had that with him, too.

Justin comes walking in, holding Jack's hand.

"Jack, here's your little sister," Justin says, approaching slowly.

"Her name is Elyze," I say, gently putting his hand on her.

"Yze," Jack says, intrigued, touching her hand gently, and then her face.

Justin says, "It's your little sister. You need to take care of her, so be gentle. She's only a baby."

We all laugh and contemplate the beauty of this magical family moment; Justin and me, our boy, and our girl. The four of us. Our family is finally complete.

On the first day, I have to wake Elyze up to feed her, because she's too tired and still quite small, but she gets better after a couple of days. Unfortunately, she has jaundice. She doesn't need to be under the UV lamp, but we have to stay at the hospital, so she can be monitored until it's gone. I can't wait to bring her back home. I miss Jack. He's been coming with Justin every night after day care pickup. He's curious, a bit bored, and keen to have his mummy back. He's a little scared to touch his sister, like she's a small animal in his eyes. I want all of us to be together at home, and I hope Elyze will be good to leave soon, especially since I have my PET scan on Friday.

As I fall asleep, I have the beautiful faces of Jack and Elyze in mind. Elyze is blonde with blue eyes, and looks like me. I'm so happy I got what I wanted. It's really a miracle, and I hope I'll get what I want most of all: a long and cancer-free life. They will give me the strength to fight. I finally have the family I've always wanted, and nothing will take that away from me, not even this disease. I feel so lucky to have met Justin. What a coincidence. It was fate for sure.

If my sister hadn't met her half-Australian first love, she would never have wanted to go to Australia or talked to me about it. If I hadn't studied my Bachelor of Business online with La Trobe Bendigo in Australia, lost my job, broken up with my boyfriend, and felt the urge to realise my dreams, I may never have wanted to see this country with my own eyes. And finally, if I hadn't met those French girls in Brisbane, the city my twin sister recommended, I would never have worked at the AB Hotel in Glebe where I met Justin. With time, I've come to the conclusion that meeting him was a miracle.

I somehow found the strength within me to go against everyone and follow my heart. Our relationship is the results of so many elements, that if any part of it had even been slightly changed, the course of our lives would have been different, and we might never have met. We were born twenty thousand kilometres apart and were finally united by a spiral of coincidences. It was like all the elements in my life, good or bad, had resulted us coming together. We were meant to be together.

On Friday, I bring my baby home with me. She lost a hundred and sixty grams the first two days but has stayed stable since then. She's taking ages to feed, at least an hour, but I'm used to it—like brother, like sister. The jaundice is still there, but feeding her every three hours should help. I don't want to go through the craziness of trying the breast and then expressing and bottle feeding. Anyway, I won't be breastfeeding too long, because I'll have to do my cancer treatment soon. So if she struggles after ten minutes, I'll bottle-feed her. Jack had been distressed by my absence and was waking up every night, so I can't wait to start our new routine and have my boys back.

At 11:30 a.m., I arrive at St Vincent hospital in Darlinghurst for my PET scan. Justin leaves me there, since the kids can't stay because of the radioactivity. The doctor calls my name, and I follow him into a small room, where he asks me the routine questions, tests my blood sugar, weighs me, and places a cannula on top on my right hand. Then he asks me to take off my clothes, put on a gown, and wait in another room.

There, I lie on a bed, underneath a warm blanket, while a nurse gives me a contrast to drink. It tastes metallic. She comes back with a syringe and the isotope to inject, placed in a protective system, and then goes behind a thick metallic board and proceeds to give me the injection. It looks dangerous, and I'm a bit scared of all this radioactivity being transferred into my body, but I have no choice. I need to know what I'm up against. I drink three more glasses of contrast, twenty minutes apart.

While lying there, I have all the time to think about what's happening to me, how the nightmare started, the lump, the delivery, and my beautiful Elyze. I hope I'm not at stage IV and that this experimental treatment will work, so I can care for my children without issues, keep my strength, and remain positive. My children are such a blessing. They're so beautiful and amazing, so fragile and young.

After an hour, I follow the nurse into another room, in which sits a big cylindrical machine. I lie down where she tells me to, and she places some kind of fabric around my arms to keep them from moving. Then, she leaves me alone. Once the door is closed, they start the machine. My eyes are closed, but I can feel it going backward into the big cylinder. It's noisy, and I must stay still. It lasts forty minutes, going back and forth slowly. They're reading my body, and soon I'll know.

Once the machine stops, I get changed, and they remove my cannula. The results are printed on a CD fifteen minutes later, and I can leave. I won't be able to breastfeed for the next six hours, and I can't see my babies for at least four. I decide to walk through Darlinghurst to get to the Kings Cross train station. On my way, I see an old church and enter to find no one else there. I pray and beg for my life before lighting a candle and leaving a note in the book of prayers. I hope someone has heard me. My heart is broken by sadness and fear, and I'm so scared of what the results will be. When I finally get home, I'm so glad to hold my baby again, laugh with Jack, and kiss my husband. They are all my life. I love them so much.

We spend the weekend enjoying our new life as four. It feels so good to have the family I've always dreamed of. I can't believe I got what I wanted. I'm so spoiled. Since I arrived in Australia five years ago, I've obtained every single thing I wanted. From finding the love of my life, staying in Australia, and obtaining a good marketing position, to having a boy who looks like Justin and a girl with my eyes and hair. I've been so blessed, so lucky. The mind is a powerful thing. I believe that focusing on what I wanted to create in my life, and visualising myself into this reality with every cell of my being and at the deepest level of my mind, has brought them to me. The law of attraction works. I want to survive this and live. I don't want to be greedy, but I really need this, too. Not just for me, but for my family.

On Monday, we have another appointment with my oncologist at the Melanoma Institute Australia in Crows Nest. Justin and I sit holding hands. Baby Elyze is in the pram next to us, and Jack is at day care.

After welcoming Elyze and praising her beauty, the doctor becomes serious.

"We've got the PET scan results...and unfortunately, it's not what we expected."

"So... do you mean I'm at stage four?"

"Yes. There are metastases in both your armpits, as well as your collarbone, spine, tailbone. and pelvic bones. The cancer is aggressive and spreading rapidly."

I turn to Justin, desperate as I try to hold back my tears. Our worst nightmare is now real. I knew it, somehow. I could feel it in my bones, literally. That was the reason my tailbone was so sore after the delivery. It was the bloody melanoma. But I do feel lucky that my brain is still intact.

Justin and I are devastated. Our world is falling apart all over again. It's the worst-case scenario. I can't bear the thought of not being there for my babies, and when I look at my newborn in the pram, I burst into tears. A relieving gasp comes from my guts that I've been holding onto all weekend. I know I'll just have to fight this, and I'm terrified.

At least we know all the facts, so we can start treatment as soon as possible. After letting the tears out of my system, with Justin's arms around me, the doctor gives me tissues. I wipe my eyes and try to compose myself.

"So now what are my options? What kind of treatment is available?" I don't want to ask about my prognosis, which will only make me feel worse. I need to kill this thing before it kills me.

"You just missed out on an immunotherapy clinical trial, but at your stage, there are two targeted treatments on a Pharmaceutical Benefits Scheme (PBS), partially refunded by Medicare. The standard treatment for a BRAF mutant patient like you, is a combination of Trametinib and Dabrafenib. This is what you could have been given for the stage III clinical trial, and it will shrink the tumours."

We're also hoping to get you into another immunotherapy trial as soon as one comes up, because usually patients develop a resistance to this treatment after nine months.

The other option is immunotherapy with Keytruda, which boosts your immune system to kill the cancer. Though only fifty percent of patients respond to this treatment, some of them are now clear of the disease. Unfortunately, you can't get it straight away unless you pay for it, because Medicare will only issue a refund if the first treatment stops working."

"How much does Keytruda cost?"

"It's expensive, about eight thousand dollars just for one infusion. You also need to add the hospital costs, so for one injection, you're looking at about seventeen thousand dollars. You'll have to get an infusion every three weeks, and we don't know how long you're going to need them for, or if it will even work on you."

"Okay then," I said. "I guess I don't have much choice in the matter. I'll take the targeted therapy."

"At least you can start the treatment today. And it works on ninety percent of patients, shrinking the tumours by at least fifty percent. The statistics are good compared to Keytruda, which only works on one out of two patients. So you should see your tumours shrink quickly. And as soon as there's an immunotherapy trial available, I'll let you know, as it works better if it's taken early on."

"I hope there's going to be a clinical trial soon."

"I know it's disappointing to be at stage IV, but at the same time, we now have two standard treatments, which wasn't the case five years ago. Research progresses fast, so it's a good time to have melanoma!" she said with a half-smile.

"Well, I guess I have to slow it down, so I can still be there when they find a cure!" I say, looking at my daughter.

"You have a beautiful baby girl…"

"I'm so worried I won't be here for her." I struggle to articulate my words as a lump of pain forms in my throat.

"Listen," she says looking me in the eye. "We're going to do our best to save you. Everything will be fine."

"Really?"

"I'll try my best, I promise." She smiles, and it reassures me.

That's all I had to hear. I will hold on to that sentence forever, as if it's the promise of survival. Though the odds are against me, I have to believe it.

I think about my life and all the things I've done so far, and realise how much I've accomplished in only five years: skydiving, flying by myself to Australia, backpacking, picking in the midst of brown snakes, going on a road trip, surfing, getting married, snorkelling on the Great Barrier Reef, bungee jumping, being pregnant three times, losing a baby, giving birth to a wonderful little boy and gorgeous baby girl, and… having terminal cancer.

With the birth of my children, I also discover that my family, the people I love the most, are my home. I have to write a bucket list again. All my dreams have come true, and even though my life is at stake, I still have new dreams to fulfil. But I feel pressured for time. The most beautiful of my goals may not become reality, but I will commit to accomplishing the impossible ones, which revolve around having conversations with my kids. I will fight for them, and I will be strong. I have no other choice but to survive.

My treatment begins tonight.

10

This Christmas will be Elyze's first but may be my last. The season is supposed to be such a happy time, but it's difficult for someone on death row. I feel like I'm a bomb ready to explode, because I just don't know when it's going to happen. I'm a control freak, and living in such uncertainty is overwhelming and stressful, so I try to act on the few things I can still control.

I research a lot online about melanoma, trying to get as much information as possible on all the treatments available and potential future progress. It's scary. All these people with cancer dying around me who are writing blogs. Desperate people…like I am. I've actually been advised by my oncologist not to follow these people, as she said that sometimes it's better to stay in denial. She's probably right.

When I stop looking and focus on positive statistics and hopeful stories, I feel a bit better. Yet, I'm not ignoring the darkness of my situation. I'm working on accepting the morbid potential outcome, so I start a list of things to do before it's too late. Some of them are already a work in progress:

- *Give a hug to my big sister, who's been a stranger since Mum's stroke*
- *Renew my vows in a church, with my family, and have a wedding cake*

- *Baptise Elyze*
- *Go on a "proper" honeymoon*
- *Exercise again and lose at least 10 Kg of my pregnancy weight*
- *- Show my country to my kids and introduce them to all my family and friends*
- *Meet my nephews and be there to watch my kids playing with them*
- *Go to Uluru*
- *Get my paperwork in order*
- *Take surfing lessons*
- *Eat at the restaurant of the Opera House I saw the first day I visited Sydney*
- *Live in a house with a pool*
- *Go to New York and see the Empire State building, Central Park, and the Statue of Liberty*
- *Cover up my old tattoo*
- *Go on a cruise*
- *Travel around the world*
- *Discover Kakadu National Park*
- *Visit San Francisco, Las Vegas, the Great Canyon, and Niagara Falls*
- *Go to Vietnam, Thailand, Bali, and New Caledonia*
- *Write a book*
- *See my kids get married*
- *Become a grandma*

It's a lot. I'm not sure I can do it all, but I'll try my best. I start by organising the most important and easily achievable ones.

But first, I need to help my parents prepare for their visit. They'll be spending a few months here. It's a lucky break that the flat underneath ours is available, and I hope we can get it before anyone else does. It will be convenient to have them so close while still maintaining some privacy, as they will stay for quite a while this time.

I've been requesting their support for a couple of weeks. I think they're in complete denial of my terminal condition and are not ready to accept that I may die at any time.

Once they confirm they're coming the last week of November, I immediately begin preparing everything. I'm excited and want them to really feel at home. After renting the flat for them, I treat it for pests and get all the furniture necessary to fill up the two bedrooms. It was a good thing Stéphanie's in-laws were getting rid of their guest house furniture. Perfect timing. I'm exhausted from the side-effects of my treatment and the sleepless nights nursing Elyze, but I'm happy. I'll soon have my parents by my side. However, due to them staying for such a long time, they will have to renew their tourist visa.

The night they arrive, we hug and kiss strongly, all grateful to see each other again, despite the circumstances. The kids are already in bed, but my parents want to see them. I let them peek in, and they agree their grandchildren are beautiful.

They're relieved to be here, closer to me and thankful for the flat arrangements. I feel I need to show them my PET scan for them to acknowledge the damage. But even after seeing all the black spots in my body that show where the tumours are, I'm not sure they understand. I can't blame them, and I don't want to hurt them. But in order to get the kind of real support I need, they have to fully comprehend the reality of the situation. Also, if it all hits the fan, I want them to be prepared. It's not a holiday trip. I'm not the kind of person who asks for help, but for the sake of my kids, I have to, and it scares me to tears.

During the second week of December 2015, Elyze has a forty-degree fever and is shaking uncontrollably. She freaks me out so much, that I bring her to the Emergency Department of St. George's hospital straight away. Apparently, she didn't cope well with the immunisation, but to be sure, the nurses take her blood and urine sample, and they also perform a lumbar puncture to rule out meningitis. It's awful to see her crying and screaming while they attempt four times to put a big needle into her little spine. I ask for another nurse, or maybe a doctor, because this one is shaking so much that she will miss another time for sure. I can't stand what I see and can't even believe this nurse hasn't given up yet or asked for help. It feels like an eternity. I'm trying to comfort my poor little girl, only six weeks old, screaming and crying in pain. They finally get the sample, and we're admitted to the children's ward at four in the morning. Thank God I have a bed and not one of those crappy folding bed seats you usually get.

This is when I start feeling the side-effects of my treatment. What timing. I really don't need this right now. After they put a cannula on Elyze and give her a drip of antibiotics, it's 5:30 a.m., and I finally go to bed. I'm shivery, extremely cold, exhausted, and nauseated. It's not the first time, and I know what to do, but the eight blankets they give me don't help. I take some painkillers, hoping for my fever to drop. It's the only thing I can do, unfortunately. By nine a.m, I've only slept an hour, and Elyze is awake.

So far, I've had these side-effects nearly every ten days, despite taking steroids daily to avoid them. They consist of a high fever, shivers, joint pain, being incredibly cold, and pretty much feeling like I have the worst flu ever. When it happens, the only thing I can do is take painkillers and wait it out. Then I have to cease the treatment for a couple of days. I've stopped it so often that I wonder if it's still working. But when I call Anna, my nurse, she explains that the treatment may actually work even better after a break, because it would sort of shock my body once I take it again. I'm hoping so, anyway.

One night, I had another side-effect. I was itchy everywhere, scratching myself to the point of bleeding. It was horrible, and I had to take antihistamines to get over it. Otherwise, the only annoying thing about this treatment is that I have to take it an hour before, and two hours after, ingesting food. So I take the tablets when I wake up and can't have my coffee for another hour. Being a mum, I have a hard time not getting my caffeine first thing in the morning. But my life depends on this treatment, so it's with a small price to pay.

Anna tells me to stay off my tablets for a couple of days, as I have a low white blood cell count. I've been tired all day, waking up just to feed Elyze and calm her down when her fever picks up. She's doing good, feeding well, and still so pretty. My parents are coming over for a couple of hours, so I can rest a bit. Justin comes in the afternoon to bring us some fresh clothes, and we both take a nap. It was a short night for him, too. He left the emergency department at one a.m., because he had to be at work in four hours. After visiting me, he picks up Jack at day care.

I'm missing nice Justin. He's been so short with me lately, taking everything the wrong way. I wish he would just hold me tight in his arms and kiss me softly. But he seems preoccupied, under pressure, stressed, and overtired. He's always on his phone with his Facebook group, talking about his remote-control cars and forgetting what's really important—his family and spending quality time with us. Or maybe it's his way of dealing with everything that's going on. I don't want him to learn his lesson the hard way, like I did.

Elyze is fine. She doesn't have meningitis. As predicted, she just a bad reaction to the vaccine, probably due to a cold. I want to get out of this children's ward that I know all too well. After our experience with Jack, everyone knows us here.

As I'm waiting to be discharged, I watch a touching documentary about people who've experienced after-death or spirit encounters. One is about a young lady who can see or hear her nana at difficult times. She'd had a strong relationship with her while alive. Her nephew had been born at twenty-five weeks and unfortunately didn't survive long after birth. She explained that her nana was there to take him when it was time. This story gives me hope that at least if I don't make it, I may still be able to see my kids grow up and somehow be there for them and Justin.

Before I left France, I'd had constant bad luck and actually thought someone had put a curse on me. Anyway, I was desperate for change and went to see a work colleague's friend, who was a clairvoyant in her spare time. I remember she told me that I would live very far away. She also said that my grandma, who'd recently passed away at the time, was with us and was watching over me, like a guardian angel. I was close to my grandma. She'd been a second mum to me ever since my mum's stroke, so I got emotional, but I was happy to know she was by my side. The woman also told me that I could speak out loud and ask my grandma for help, because she could hear me. Since then, I've prayed with Grandma Denise and asked for her help to stay on Earth, with my family, my husband, my kids, and also my parents and my twin. I've told her how I'm sure I'd be an awesome angel, but I'm an even better mum. I let her know I have to stay here and that I'm willing to do whatever it takes. I'm sure she's listening.

I remember my grandma so well; her smell, her cheeky grin, her kindness and all her stories. After my mum's stroke, she'd come to our house every afternoon. She always said she felt guilty and would repeatedly say how it should have happened to her instead.

Mum would spend her time brooding over her sad situation, so we wanted her to have a hobby to do in her spare time. With my grandma's help, we managed to convince her to water paint again, with her left hand this time. After a slow start and lots of opposition, we were happy to see Mum enjoying something again. Of course, it was hard, and she got frustrated many times, but overall, she learned to be more patient. It was therapeutic and gave her the motivation to get better. She kept improving, until it got to the point you wouldn't believe she'd ever been right-handed, though writing and talking remained a struggle.

"Mamie" Denise, as I used to call her, became my confidant. I could nearly tell her everything. We got to know each other better while revealing our personal stories, and she used to love giving me advice on men and relationships. She was a modern woman for her time.

She was born on February 2, 1922, so obviously, her favourite number was two. She'd been through the Second World War and told me so many stories about it. At the end of the war, she married my Grandpa Charles, who'd been trapped in a German forced labour camp for years.

She told me how she'd organised her wedding, paying for her shoes with food tickets, and that she'd started working at sixteen years old as a secretary for an insurance company. She'd talk about how everyone used to love her handwriting and her joy of being the mum to her four beautiful daughters. But she also told me how my grandpa made bad business decisions as a real estate developer, and the whole family ended up living with her parents.

My grandpa died when I was four years old, so I have no memories of him. Just a black-and-white picture from when he was in his forties. He was a good-looking man, blond with blue eyes, and he loved to paint. Grandma Denise told me that when she found out he was cheating on her with one of her girlfriends, she figured the best way to get rid of the mistress was to bring them together more often. So she organised all these lunches with the two of them, and my grandpa got so irritated that he asked my grandma to stop inviting her. They never saw the bestie again and never divorced. But Grandpa Charles left their home to be with a sugar mummy, who let him paint as much as he wanted. Grandma eventually let him come back because he was broke, and she probably still loved him. However, she could never forgive him, so he wound up sleeping in the kids' bedroom, where he died of a heart attack in his fifties.

We used to go for a cup of tea together in the city centre of Nice. One day, she took me to my favourite ice cream café, even though she couldn't afford it. She was so happy to please me. She always used to say, *"We only live once!"* it was her way of justifying indulging ourselves from time to time.

My grandma witnessed the beginning of a mass-consumption society, discovering life with a car, TV, and fridge. Before these inventions, she'd had to walk to a special place to get ice, so they could keep the food for a few days. She'd also go to the river to wash their clothes and dirty diapers by hand. Then after the war, everything became accessible, and she told me stories about how revolutionary it was. I could picture everything like I was there. It was magical. I loved her so much.

She definitely taught me a thing or two about men, but the best lesson she ever taught me was that women should never chase a man. That was probably the mistake I'd been making with one man after another… until the day I decided to follow her advice when I met Justin.

Without my grandma by our side for the rough beginning of our new "normal" with Mum, I'm not sure I would have coped that well. Every time I had to tell someone about my mum, I used to fall into tears, and it took me a while to get over this tragic event.

The day I lost my grandma, I felt like my world had fallen into bits, leaving a big hole inside me. It was 2004. I was twenty-two years old, studying in Montpellier, and in a long-distance relationship with a man named Romain. We stayed together for eight months of ups and downs, though he did cheat on me multiple times. After we'd been apart for a while, I decided to give our relationship another chance and really thought we were back together for good. When I found out I was wrong, the news was particularly devastating, by virtue of the timing.

On the first Friday of February, I woke up suddenly at seven a.m. and felt the urge to go back to Nice. I called Romain, and he agreed to come with me. After a day of unexplained dreadful feelings that something wasn't quite right, I picked him up after class, and we arrived in Nice that night. Laetitia, who'd been living in Paris at the time, was spending the week at my parents' flat, but nobody was home when I got there. Anxious, I called her. She answered in a state of tears and told me the devastating news—Grandma Denise had passed away that morning around seven a.m.

My entire body was overtaken by shivers, and I couldn't talk anymore. I was in shock as I drove to my grandma's, trying to see through the tears. I couldn't digest the news. It was too sudden, too soon, too painful. I cried uncontrollably, like I'd just lost my mother. I was inconsolable.

When I arrived, I discovered that my dad had placed her in her bed after the doctor had confirmed her death. They'd found her in her shower, where she must have fallen over that morning. They told me that she hadn't wanted to receive another pacemaker when her last one had given out. I knew she was tired after living a full life and that she wanted to go, but I didn't think I'd lose her so early. I still needed her. I still wanted her in my life. There I was, in her bedroom, desperate and in tears, looking at her lying in her bed as if she was asleep. She seemed so calm and rested, a small lamp on her bedside table lighting the room. I cried as I took her in my arms, kissing her cold cheek, desperate to feel her move again. I was too late; I didn't have a chance to say goodbye.

That weekend, I spent my time comforting my mum and my sister and helping Dad prepare everything for the funeral. I was in such pain. I could feel the ball of sorrow forming deep in my gut that came out through my tears. I didn't have much time for Romain, but he seemed to understand, and after four days I knew why. Despite standing beside me throughout my grandmother's funeral, and a long three-hundred-kilometre drive, I discovered he'd been cheating on me with his ex, the one who'd so coldly dumped him prior to our relationship. She'd come back into his life… and he'd chosen her over me. When it was time for me to leave, I drove through the cold rainy night in a flood of sadness, grief, and anger, back to my lonely student apartment in Montpellier.

I'd just lost two important people. I couldn't help feeling upset and ashamed that Romain had even been by my side while I buried my grandma, because she would have hated what he'd done to me. I gave him no more chances to repair our relationship. It was just over. I figured that I'd been the one giving my all to this relationship. It was like I was rowing the boat alone, so we were going around in circles. A relationship can't be successful without a team effort.

It was so hard to deal with grieving my "Mamie" by myself. I had my friends, but I didn't want to be sad with them. I needed them to help me move on. The next months were tough for me, but since that day, I've felt like she's always been by my side, because even in the worst situations, I've always had some sort of luck.

11

I've started seeing a psychologist. I don't feel depressed, and I definitely don't want to die, but I'm anxious. I can't stop thinking, and my brain's been messing with me. The doctor teaches me the basics of mindfulness and meditation, and even if it doesn't save me, it's saving my soul from the darkness of cancer. The medical side may be painful to live with, but the emotional roller coaster is even worse.

One of the most important things I'm learning is that just because my brain wants to talk, doesn't mean I have to listen. I can just say, "Oh, interesting" and move on. I don't have to hold on to every thought and analyse them all. I can just acknowledge them and let them be, as ignoring them worsens the problem. I can't let my brain and my thoughts bully me. This brings me great relief.

I start to meditate daily, do deep breathing, and scan my body, visualising it as healthy, with no tumours or dark spots anywhere, and find peace in bringing myself back to a meditative state when it starts to wander. My anxiety decreases, and I'm better able to cope with my emotions. The mind is so powerful, that I prefer to have it on my side, strengthening me with positive thoughts, rather than having it bring me down with my deepest and darkest negative ones.

Living mindfully and being in present also helps me appreciate every detail of my life.

My psychologist also tells me that it's normal for me to go through the five stages of grieving my own life: denial, anger, bargaining, depression, and acceptance. But I'm not sure I've been through any of them so far, except maybe denial.

It's nearly Christmas, and my wishes this year aren't materialistic at all. As I get older, they get more intangible and even harder to obtain. This year, I have only one: to get cured and live a long healthy and happy life with my children and my love. I hope that my grandma, my guardian angel, will help me get through it all.

I'm glad my parents are with us for Elyze's first Christmas, like they were also here for Jack's. They've already come to Australia three times in four years. I'm thankful to have them. They love me, and they show it. Mum can barely walk. Her right arm hasn't moved much in twenty years, and she doesn't understand a word of English. Dad pushes her in her cheap and now quite dangerous wheelchair, and with his lymphoma, he's been dealing with doctors, as well.

Jack's grown so much in a year, and since they met our beautiful Elyze, they've been under her spell. They take her into their flat when I feel too tired to nurse her at night, and Dad wakes up to feed her. It's a big effort for him, because he loves his sleep, but Elyze is easier than Jack was. She feeds in ten minutes now and goes back to sleep straight away. And it's also easier to put her to bed. No rocking or patting necessary. She's the best baby ever, which is such a relief with my exhaustion. If she was as difficult as Jack used to be, it would have been a lot harder to cope. I'm telling you, there is a God. Also, Mum and Dad keep her while I go to my doctor appointments. She's better off playing at home than being trapped in the car for hours and visiting the Melanoma Institute clinics.

I'm glad we're celebrating together and that we don't have to work too hard on the menu this time. We love our traditional Christmas Eve, so we'll have French fat liver and smoked salmon for the entrée. Justin's dad comes with Belinda, and they bring a beautiful lamb shoulder and roasted pork leg, with beans and potatoes on the side. Then we have a delicious cheese platter and make a great chocolate "log" for dessert. There are lit candles, and a big table is placed in the middle of our flat for everyone to feast around.

Everybody seems so normal. They don't feel the urge to live in the moment, because they don't have to. I feel lucky somehow, as I believe I'm even more thankful to have them around me on Christmas Eve and appreciate every second of them. Every detail is here. I can see everything and capture the magic of the moment as if time has slowed down. I feel like I'm outside of my body, looking at the scenery. It's beautiful, and I love it. I'm now living mindfully, every single day and repeat my grandma's mantra to myself: *We only live once.*

But when everyone leaves, and I'm alone with my husband as we sit in front of the Christmas tree, I can't help telling him how I really feel. "What if it's my last Christmas, Justin? I can't stand this idea. I barely know Elyze, and Jack is still so young." I burst into tears as I reach for the comfort of his arms.

"Don't say stupid things like that. It won't be your last Christmas," he says, trying to reassure me.

"How do you manage to remain so calm and confident all the time?"

"Because I know it. You will have many more Christmases. Remember, you have no choice."

"I know, love. I'm sorry to put you in such a bad place. I want to be here to help you with the kids. It will be so hard for you otherwise."

"You will, because I don't know what I'd do, either." He's now sobbing with me.

"Oh Justin. I'm so scared they won't remember their mummy…"

"I'm sure you'll be here. You will live a long life. Stay positive."

"How do you know?"

"I know, because I made a deal," he says with confidence.

"What are you talking about?"

"I told whoever is in charge up there that they had to swap my life with yours. I promised that if they let you live, I'd take your place. So if one of us has to go, it will be me."

"You're silly. It doesn't work like that. Your life is as important as mine, and the kids need you as much as they need me. I love you. And I want you to live. You can't just trick the system like that. Stop making that request, please."

"No, I won't. It's a balance thing. If one life needs to go, it has to be mine. The kids need you more than they need me, and I want you to live."

"I want you to live, too. No one is going to die. Please stop," I beg.

"Don't worry. You're going to annoy the crap out of me forever." He laughs.

"I hope I will."

"You will. I'm sure of it," he says, holding me tight in his arms.

The kids have been spoiled by Santa, and Jack loves getting presents. He also starts to understand what Christmas is about. Every time we see a nativity scene, I talk about Jesus, Mary, and Joseph. So now when he sees one, he asks where Jesus is. I tell him that he could ask anything of Jesus, and if it comes from his heart, Jesus will help him. Deep down, I'm praying that I'll be saved. I have to survive for my kids and my husband. Jesus can't call me back now, because it's terrible timing. He has to wait at least until the kids are in school, so it will be a little easier on Justin. But if I'm being honest, I want Him to wait until my kids have kids themselves.

We celebrate New Year's Eve at home, watching the amazing Sydney fireworks on the big screen, sipping a small glass of Champagne, and then cheering and kissing at the end of the countdown.

In early January, I go to my PET scan, followed by a CT scan and oncologist appointment. To my delight, we discover the medicine is working. One of my tumours can't be seen anymore, and the two big ones in each armpit have significantly reduced in size. The rest are inactive. Having tumours with no activity is good, because it means the cancer is under control, and it's like you don't have it anymore. Of course, if all the tumours disappeared, it would be even better.

I'm not eligible for the next clinical trial, because this particular one is for people who never had treatment. If I'd waited, I'd be dead by now. But the news isn't too bad at all. More clinical trials will come up towards March or April, and we're hoping I can start one of them.

Meanwhile, I have to tick the boxes off my bucket list, so I go for two surf lessons within the next two weeks. I haven't touched a board since shortly after arriving in Sydney, and I really want to be able to take a wave without falling once. And I make it happen. It's exhausting doing the washing machine again, but now that I've learned about the rips on a beginner board, it's easier. I feel so free and revitalised again and have a wonderful time. It's great to do something for myself for once. I love it, and I leave Cronulla Beach with a big smile on my face and a happy mood.

I also start exercising again. After nearly two years of pregnancies, I'm keen to regain my body shape and get my energy and self-confidence back. I gained nearly twelve kilos with Elyze, and I can't stand myself anymore. I'm feeling heavy and uncomfortable in my skin, which doesn't help my fight against the black beast. One thing's for sure: it's hard. Exercising is demanding, and losing weight while on steroids is tough. But I need the drugs to limit the side-effects of my treatment, so I can stay on it longer. Breastfeeding would have helped a little, like it did after Jack's birth. I never got big with Jack, though. I didn't have the chance to, because he was in a rush to see the world.

I find a great venue for Elyze's baptism and the renewal of our vows. It's a gorgeous little cottage in Peakhurst, with beautiful gardens full of roses and flowers and a charming fountain. I've ordered my dress, custom-made in China again. It's a light pink sleeveless one this time, with a gorgeous ruffle organza gown. It's beautiful. I just have to order the cake, prepare the music, and send the invites. Then, it will be sorted. Finally, I will have a proper reception for our wedding. The one we had five years ago was beautiful, but my family wasn't there, and I'm happy to be able to make up for it, especially since we never managed to have the wedding in France. I'm so glad to have my parents and my twin sister by my side as I marry my love.

Justin and I didn't go far on our first honeymoon. With our wedding being on Valentine's Day weekend, it would be way too expensive to fly that week, so we decide to go to Hamilton Island a few days beforehand. It will be our first real holiday since we went to Europe after the loss of our first baby, two and half years ago. It seems like forever. Being on a tropical island by ourselves, for four days and three nights of cruises, cocktails by the pool, relaxation, and snorkelling on the reef with no distractions, sounds like heaven. I can't wait to conquer my husband again and have some desperately needed quality time together. It will be short, but without the kids, time will feel longer for sure.

Also, as Mum and Dad will be with us until the end of April, I decide to tick another item off my bucket list: Uluru. My sister will help with the kids while we're on Hamilton Island, but for Uluru, she won't be here anymore, and my parents will have to manage alone. Since Jack will go to day care, I plan to leave on a Monday and come back on Friday afternoon, so they just have to deal with him mornings and evenings.

Elyze is still quite young and will be super easy to take care of during the day. I'm ecstatic. We will enjoy a helicopter flight over Uluru and Kata Juta and rent a car to go to the rocks and back to the resort. I also plan for a romantic dinner by the stars for our last night.

I'm trying to make the most out of the time I have left. I start to wonder if I did well organising the wedding and holidays when money is running out, but these ticks are events to look forward to and help me feel better. Also, this has all made me realise how big the gap is between what I've done in my life and what I want to achieve before the end of it. Once I've completed most of my list, I'll feel more peaceful. I know I can't make all my wishes happen immediately, such as owning our own house, as prices in Sydney are ridiculously expensive, but I can realise most of them.

I have to fight. Nowadays, with new treatments and clinical trials, things can change. They have to. I will defy the odds. I have to survive for my babies.

Elyze is helping me as much as she can, since she's now sleeping twelve hours straight through the night. She's always so happy and smiley. She gives me all the positive waves I need for a good start to my day.

When my beautiful twin sister finally lands in Australia, I'm so happy to be able to take her in my arms. She's always been my rock, my anchor. It's quite an emotional reunion due to the circumstances, and she falls into tears when we talk about my prognosis s. But she's happy with my results and that I'm responding well to the treatment. I tell her that I won't be rushed into any clinical trials, as my oncologist would rather make sure I do the one with the best chance. Because once I start, I may not be able to go back on my regimen.

Laetitia is glad to meet her niece and nephew for the first time. She thinks they're cute and is looking forward to spending some time with them. I explain to Jack and Elyze who she is and that Mummy and Daddy will be away for a few days. Jack doesn't seem to understand, and he's quite clingy before we take off.

Laetitia is a mum to three kids, and I'm sure she'll take care of my babies like they were her own. I also hope Jack won't drive her mad with his tantrums. He's experiencing the terrible twos. I can't wait to enjoy more time with my sister once we return. She's grown out her hair, so it's the same length as mine now. We look so much alike, Jack and Elyze will probably think she's me. I explain to my sister their routine and how to handle them, and we're off.

Justin and I have a magical time on the tropical island. I'd been hoping for a relaxing, romantic, and bonding quality time with my dear husband, and I'm not disappointed.

We arrive on Tuesday and enjoy an afternoon soaking and drinking cocktails at the pool bar. Then we watch the sunset on a catamaran and savour a nice dinner in a Mexican restaurant on the marina. The next morning, we go on a cruise to Whitehaven beach, one of the most beautiful beaches of Australia, and it's amazing. It's hot, and the sand burns our feet, but swimming in the light blue ocean and admiring the panorama is extraordinary, even if we have to wear a complete stinger suit because of the jellyfish. We also have a scary close encounter with a wild giant dragon lizard.

After another afternoon relaxing by the pool bar—definitely our favourite—we go to the Tavern pub for a chicken parmigiana dinner. Snorkelling on the reef is cancelled for the next day, so I have to check what else we can do to get a similar experience. There's no way we're not seeing Heart Reef. I arrange to go on an all-day cruise on Bait Reef, with a helicopter flight over Heart Reef. We just have to rush to get the flight in, as it must be booked onboard only.

In the afternoon, we act like teenagers, playing a weird bowling game called Kegels, with nine pins placed in a diamond shape and balls with only two holes, which definitely kills our arms and fingers, but we have so much fun.

Then we snooze in our bedroom before going on the Denison Star Dinner cruise at 5:30 p.m. at the marina. This is such an awesome dining experience. It's one of the best nights we've had in a long time.

After a delicious three-course tasting diner, in which we describe each dish like two food experts on a mission, we watch the sunset drinking a beer, sitting side by side, Justin's arm around my shoulders. Then we finish the date night looking at the stars, wrapped in each other's arms, kissing.

On our last day, we have to wake up early to depart for a fantastic cruise on the Great Barrier Reef. Afterward, we fly twenty minutes over Hardy Reef, Bait Reef, and Heart Reef, which is only sixteen metres long. I'm in the co-pilot seat, enjoying the amazing views of the ocean. The waters are so clear that we can see the asperities of the reefs and observe a continent of corals.

After a quick lunch, we spend two hours snorkelling hand in hand, watching the colourful coral and all sorts of fishes. It's beautiful. No turtles this time. We were lucky to swim with them when we'd gone on a reef cruise outside Cairns years ago. But there's so many more fish this time. At the end of the day, we're exhausted and savour some Greek specialties with a few beers for our dinner at the Mantra Bay Restaurant on the marina. It's the last night before having the kids again, and we enjoy every minute of it. Having some time for ourselves is great, but I'm glad I'll soon be with my babies again. I've missed them and my sister, too.

We had trouble avoiding the cancer talk during our holiday, and one emotional night, I tell Justin I want to tick another two items off my bucket list: to pass my citizenship test and move from our flat to a house. We need more space with two babies, and it's stressful to put them to bed in the same bedroom. Also, a little backyard would be awesome for them to play in, especially if my health worsens. I wouldn't have to keep them trapped inside or go out to the park. We could stay in our own backyard. Of course, we're going to rent and not buy, but our budget is tight, so it will be difficult to find a house in our Rockdale area for around five hundred dollars a week. But I want to get out of our flat. I'm suffocating.

With only Justin's wages, it's tough to pay for everything, and we have to take from our small savings every month. I hope we can get a bit of help from Centrelink, and I wonder if I should try to work from home in order to make money. I'm selling every unnecessary item we have on Gumtree to make a few bucks, but it's not enough, and it's difficult to go from being the breadwinner to making nothing. I feel guilty.

However, our financial situation didn't stop me from buying a Desigual bag at seventy percent off at the Sydney Airport on our way to Hamilton Island. If you fall in love with a handbag, you have to buy it. At least, that was my justification. I'm living like there's no tomorrow, so I'm pleasing myself a bit, after all those years of sacrifice for a house we will never buy.

At first, it was the opposite. I wondered if I should buy anything, since it would be a waste if I died. Justin would have to get rid of everything…or I would, just before I went. I thought that I shouldn't waste money on me anymore, since I wouldn't last long. It was better to keep it for the kids and Justin. I was even thinking of emptying my closet and getting rid of the shoes I never wore. But then I thought I should enjoy myself and think positive. I will live a long life, and that handbag will die of being worn out before I do. I love it, and it's the first thing I've bought for myself in over two years. It put a monster smile on my face while making my dress look heaps better.

We're back in Sydney on Saturday morning, which is perfect timing to spend quality time with my babies. Apparently, Jack and Elyze really thought Laetitia was me. It's only when we return that Jack realises he's been tricked. He's been calling her "Mama" all week long. There's a look of confusion on his face as he looks at the two of us, back and forth. Then he runs toward me crying, "Mama" as if I betrayed him. I've missed the kids a lot. I was right. Four days without them seemed like two weeks. It was great to relax and enjoy some dating time with Justin, even if it was hard to avoid the baby talk. But it was nice. We had heaps of time for ourselves.

My parents leave for three days in the Blue Mountains, our Christmas present for them. They've been helping us so much, and I wanted to thank them with some relaxing time off. Also, when they went there with us, it was pouring rain. Lucky for them, this time the weather is sunny. Meanwhile, Laetitia and I prepare the final details of the baptism and wedding this weekend. When I show her the venue, she says it's beautiful. I'm so glad she can be there this time. I laugh with her when I realise that she got engaged at the same time I did, but I'm about to get married for the second time and have another child baptised, while she still hasn't fixed a date for her wedding.

I'm so happy to spend some quality time with my twin. I haven't seen her since our trip to France, and I've missed her so much. I feel complete with her around. It always feels like something is missing when she's not close to me. With Skype, Viber, emails, and the mobile phone, things are better than they were twenty years ago for sure, but having her physically with me is so much better. I can talk to her at any time. We have breakfast, lunch, and dinner together, so she's witnessing life at the same time, with my whole family.

She laughs with me and comes with me to my doctor appointments. We visit around together and have fish and chips on Watson's Bay after a nice walk on the beach. We go body boarding in Cronulla, lazing in Manly, shopping in the city. and talk like we left each other yesterday.

It's refreshing, uplifting, and energising to have her by my side. On top of that, she's an awesome help. She prepares my coffee in the morning after waking up with the kids, while I sleep in for a bit. She also dresses them up and plays with them, and they love her, naturally, as if she was me. Jack still calls her mummy as he struggles to figure out why I doubled up. It's only in the last few days that he starts calling her "Tata," which is aunty in French. With all her help, I manage to rest, so we can enjoy our days out.

We go to Kiama markets with Justin on her last Sunday with us, so she can experience life outside the big city as well. I think about how nice it would be if she lived here with her kids and partner, Mickael. We could see each other more often and raise our children together. But Mickael is in the French administration and doesn't speak very good English, while she's in payroll, and laws are so different here. On top of that, she had surgery at eighteen to remove her entire thyroid to avoid cancer and has been taking a daily treatment since, entirely financed by the French medical system.

I've been missing my family even more since I was diagnosed with cancer. I guess it put things into perspective. It's a lonely journey, and having them all here feels so good. I'm afraid to lose them again. I wonder if I'll manage without their support. I hope I'll be able to cope without damaging my health. I have to limit my stress and rest as much as I can, but without them, I'm afraid it will be difficult.

The wedding goes well, except that Jay, Justin's brother, who was supposed to be our witness and Elyze's godfather, comes in shorts. I'm shocked and hurt. Couldn't he make any effort, really? I'm so upset that I realise halfway to the church I've forgotten my flowers, and Laetitia runs back upstairs to get them. When I arrive at the church, I start panicking and can barely breathe. I decide to have Jessie for a witness, since he's Justin's stepbrother, and he's wearing a suit. It's so different from the first time. It's weird being this shaky. I know my husband now, and I love him even more. My family is here, too. I'd wanted to marry Justin in my family's presence even before my diagnosis, but this time around when the priest says, "in sickness or in health." it will definitely make more sense.

I have trouble walking down the aisle, with my shoes catching in my gown, but this time I have my dad by my side, proud of his beautiful daughter. I'm glad to arrive face to face with Justin. He's smiling.

I had returned my original ring, so he could give it to me during the ceremony, and he did the same. But when the priest asks him to put the ring on my finger, he takes his wallet out of his pocket. All I can think is, *What is he doing?* Then I realise it's the simple band I'd wanted, and I'm nearly in tears when I see the surprise ring. Yes, I got a beautiful bridal set five years ago, two thin bands of diamonds, one with a bigger diamond for the engagement ring, but it was hard to wear on a daily basis. I had to take it off to wash my hands, go for a swim, or do anything, and I wanted to be able to wear my wedding band every day and night, like my parents do. My dad can't even remove his at this point.

Justin passes it on to my finger with a big smile, satisfied with my response. After five years, three pregnancies and two kids, he's still in love with me, still keen on pleasing me, and I feel the same way.

I wrote our prayers for the wedding, and my sister reads them. It's an emotional moment for me, hearing them out loud, in front of all our loved ones and God, with me "officially" asking to be cured, so I can help my family and be there for my children. I'm so hoping that my prayers will be heard and answered.

Jack gets unsettled and wants to join us at the altar. So after renewing our vows, Jack offers me the flower he found in the garden outside and comes with us to celebrate Elyze's baptism. All of a sudden, the tension comes down, and the atmosphere feels so much more relaxed. We did it again. We got married with God and my family as witnesses.

Elyze is beautiful in her little white fancy dress and, like Jack a year ago, doesn't cry when the priest sprinkles the holy water over her forehead. All went well, except for Jay and his shorts…Grrr! Elyze looks like an angel and behaves like one, too. I'm so happy she's now part of the Christian Church and to have such a special day, surrounded by our loved ones.

We all leave the church listening to one of my favourite songs, "Somewhere Over the Rainbow" by Bob Marley, who died of melanoma the year I was born. I'm happy. It wasn't as emotional as the first wedding but still filled with love. Justin and I know each other so well now, yet he managed to surprise me. It felt so quick, too. Overall, it went even better than expected.

After a few group pictures outside the church, we all drive to the venue in Peakhurst, and everyone is pleased to discover the charming cottage, surrounded by the garden full of flowers. I planned an afternoon tea with delicious savoury and sweet bites.

After we thank everyone for coming, my sister gives a great speech about how happy she is for us and how special I am to her. Justin and I then cut the cake and dance to our song, "Throw Your Arms Around Me," by Hunters and Collectors, since we couldn't on our first wedding day. I'm so happy to have my sister, my parents, and my friends there This time around I'm surrounded by my loved ones.

I am disappointed one of my friends couldn't make it to the wedding. Under these special circumstances, I feel let down. Most people don't know how to deal with someone who has a disease, and unfortunately, you lose a lot of "friends" in the process. I think they try to avoid future pain by not watching you as you die. Maybe it wrecks their happy environment or it's hard to take something good out of a friendship with the potential loss. But I can understand, because even my parents, husband, and sister have trouble comprehending what I'm going through.

I'm glad the reception is a success, and I'm proud and happy to be married to my gentleman again. Baptising Elyze on the same day is the icing on the cake. I feel blessed to share my life with such a wonderful man. He could be grumpy sometimes, but deep down he's such a sweetheart and a generous soul.

I'm so lucky to have given birth to two beautiful children with him. They're my little miracles. Jack did everything early. He's now twenty-one months old and has all his teeth. He's running and playing soccer like a champ and is starting to go to the potty. Elyze is also a little miracle, with her being my third pregnancy, born healthy and safe following a premature baby and with me having thyroid issues and stage four melanoma. She's beautiful, with her big blue eyes, and doing so well.

I feel spoiled and blessed, living the Aussie dream with my Prince Charming. My grandma is probably watching over me. I just have to be cured to believe in fairy tales. I'm so scared to die. Sometimes I cry at night. I want to survive. I love my children and my husband so much. Though I've been blessed with three miracles already, I must have a fourth one. It has to happen. I need it in order to sustain the first three.

12

Every three weeks, I have to go for a CT scan and see my oncologist. I also do a PET scan every two months, or earlier, if necessary. The PET provides the activity rating, while the CT localises the tumours. It's mid-March, and it's that time again. I have the results of my last CT, and it's neither worse nor better. The tumour in the left armpit has grown slightly, and of course, I'm worried. My oncologist tells me it's stable, which gives me more time at least. She still wants to wait until I have no other option but to go into a clinical trial, as my treatment is keeping me stable for now. If it stops working, my next option is infusions of Keytruda, the expensive immunotherapy that works well, but only in fifty percent of patients.

Time is running out quickly, and with it, my hope. That's the scariest part. During my online research, I've discovered that when patients are told their treatment no longer works, and they don't have any options left, they usually die within three to four months. From life to death, there isn't much time. I'm thinking about my kids again. Always them. They're my reasons for living. I want to be here for them. I want to stay alive with every cell in my body. Living in uncertainty is challenging for the control freak I am, but meditation teaches me that the sky is always blue behind the clouds and storms. The dark times never stay around forever. It will be nice again at some point. I just have to remember that.

I have side-effects all week, with fevers and all the crap that goes with it, and also weird sensations in my legs. I can barely move them. They're heavy and painful. My oncologist advises another PET scan. I hate them. They take all day, I have to fast for six hours beforehand, and the hardest part is that I have to wait six hours after injection to hold my babies. But I'm glad to do it, so I know where I'm at. Information is my only ally. It's crucial.

On a positive note, Justin and I go to the Bennelong Restaurant at the Sydney Opera House. I've wanted to go there since my second day in Sydney when I looked through the glass windows to see this beautiful restaurant and imagined how amazing it would be to eat there. I knew the food would probably be delicious, and it would feel so special looking at the stars through the glass ceiling. When Uncle Gino offered us a hundred-dollar voucher for any restaurant, I chose this one. Another tick on my list.

It's such a special moment for us. Justin wears his wedding suit and city shoes for the occasion and looks handsome. I wear a lovely black dress—the only one I could still fit into—and we're two beautiful people about to enter a fancy restaurant.

The waiter welcomes us and asks if we've come for a special occasion. I don't know how to answer, and Justin and I look at each other, lost for a moment, until the waiter says, "Just celebrating life?" This answer is perfect for us, so we reply with a big, "That's it." We're happy to be placed at our table without having to mention that my life is at stake and that we're trying to tick off my entire bucket list.

The place is gorgeous. The glass ceiling reflects all the little lamps lighting the room, and it looks like the sky is full of stars. But the best part is that I get to get to spend a wonderful time with the love of my life. He's put away his phone and talks to me nicely, smiling and looking at me like when we were first dating. I fell in love with the way he used to look at me so intently. I've missed it, and I have it back. It's the most precious gift ever, and I try to reflect it back to him. He's romantic and funny, so sexy in his suit, and I feel like I did five years ago. That's the best part of it; knowing that we both really care for and love each other.

We're sitting in a booth, and while I sip on a fruity rosé, Justin savours a boutique beer. We chat and enjoy each other's company before dinner arrives. I appreciate every second of this magical night. The three-course meal is succulent. We have fun describing every sensation and the taste of each element composed on the plate. The mix of flavours is astonishing. Our palates have a fantastic time.

Afterward, we share scrumptious desserts. Justin has picked the best one, as usual. And to beautifully conclude our date, we receive a glass of champagne from our waiter. He'd had to move us to accommodate a VIP, and the staff felt sorry for us, even though we didn't really care. But we appreciate the nice gesture. The service is definitely the best I've ever had, and we love sipping on the bubbles before leaving the restaurant for a romantic walk on the harbour. We contemplate the night views of the city, like tourists, newly in love, and we're surprised to see fireworks above the Opera. It's such an amazing finish to my perfect date with my dear husband.

A week later, I get good news regarding my PET scan: the tumours are less active, even though they grew slightly, so it's not concerning. On my way back from the scan, I go to St. Mary's Cathedral. Last time I was there with Justin a couple of months ago, I lit a candle, praying for my health and my family, but hadn't made the coin donation required, because I didn't have any change. So I give back what I owe and add enough to light another candle. It's also confession time, and I wait for the priest to receive me. It takes a while, so I have a seat and think about my recent behaviour. I realise I've been quite self-absorbed lately. Justin mentioned at the restaurant that his dad didn't understand some of my behaviour, because he didn't get how difficult it was for me to deal with what I'm going through and the emotional roller coaster that comes with it. This makes me realise that I'm not sure I like the woman I'm becoming.

My life is never going to be the same anymore. Even though I'm used to change. I just feel like I've been through so many life-changing events. But this time it's different. It seems like I'm grieving my old self and becoming someone else. And that's the scariest part. I'm not the person I used to be, and I vow to try my best to love myself again.

I will change. I will open my eyes and turn towards others instead of always feeling sorry for myself. It's not just about me. Okay, I have cancer, and that sucks big time. But I can't let it define me. I'm other things, too, and my family have their own lives. They're not responsible for my disease; no one is. I'm not just a person with cancer. I'm so much more.

When the priest receives me, I tell him how bad I feel that I've been awful at times with my parents and my husband, even though they try to help me. That I recognise they're a good support system, and instead of being thankful and loving, I get upset and feel unsatisfied. As if they owe me something.

He gives me a good analogy about Jesus during his own journey to death, carrying his cross. He didn't complain. He wasn't upset. He kept loving and caring for us, never giving up. This made me understand that no matter how long we have to live, the most important thing is to love and care for those around us. As my psychologist told me, to find peace, you need to live by your values. It's the only way. So, from now on, I will try not to complain anymore and live like I'm not defined by my condition. I have to be happy again, as much as I used to be. It's been ages since my husband and I have been intimate. It's hard to find the energy and the time with two kids and my parents in the middle. Also, cancer isn't sexy for me and kind of kills the mood. But I promise myself to change that. After all of these epiphanies, I'm so grateful I made this stop at the church. It makes me feel better, and I hope that one day I'll be able to thank God for saving my life and curing me.

I think about my beautiful kids. Elyze is crying a lot lately, because she's teething, and I can have full conversations with Jack. I'm so blessed to have such a beautiful family. I need to stop fearing. I will take my head out of the sand, get my act together, and notice the beauty surrounding me. Because life is beautiful.

On Sunday, March 20, 2016, I attend my first Melanoma March, which is a yearly fundraiser organised by the Melanoma Institute Australia, and I have to speak for the occasion. So, I tell my story, the quick version of it, in front of the crowd of patients, relatives affected by melanoma, and my family. I don't give too many details, but this speech seems to echo in my dad's mind. I think it's what he needed to hear and see in order to realise this is all real. When I leave the stage to return to his side, he gives me a big hug. Then he releases a loud sigh and falls into tears, crying in my arms, like the day we buried his sister, who passed away from breast cancer. I tell him that I will be fine. I will fight my best fight, and I will win, because I have to. He says he hopes I'm right and is desperate to see me better. I'm happy my mum isn't here. The event started early, and it would have been difficult with her wheelchair. She worries too much already. I don't want her to suffer because of me.

I cut the ribbon before we start the march. It's emotional for us—Justin, Dad, and me—and all the others around us who are affected by melanoma. But we're walking through this journey one step at a time, with our kids by our side, who are enjoying life to the fullest, unaware of the sad situation. They bring the smiles back to our faces, one day at a time.

At the beginning of April, I feel better knowing that my health is stable. I'm not as depressed or sad. Dealing with uncertainty is challenging for me. The loss of control is overwhelming, so I have to do even more in order to stay as in control as I can. And somehow, I've never imagined that preparing everything for the worst-case scenario would help me as much as it does. If it all hits the fan, I may have only a couple of months, definitely not enough time to sort out all the paperwork and leave behind what I want for the kids. Plus, if I have only months left, I'd like to enjoy and appreciate every second with my kids and my family, not doing stupid paperwork and organising my funeral. I don't want my husband struggling with all the details when the time comes. He will have enough on his plate, dealing with grief and two young kids. And he hates paperwork. I'm the one in charge of his company invoices and payslips, as well as our household budget, including bills, rent, and all internet accounts. He won't know how to do a thing.

I must be ready, just in case. But merely thinking about contacting people and organising my funeral, is already overwhelming and stressful. Getting it out of the way will take that off my mind and help me believe I will have all the time in the world for the important things. One of my first tasks is to buy birthday cards for my kids. I'll take the time to write letters for each of their birthdays, until they'd be twenty-one. Then, they should be old enough to survive without mummy's wishes and advice. I'm hoping I'll be able to get rid of each letter and write on the actual card instead. But just in case, I'm covered for the next twenty years.

Having a to-do list of what needs to happen before I die seems awful, but it comforts me, because I'm in charge. I will trick Murphy's Law. I don't know if you've noticed, but it's always when you take your umbrella that it doesn't rain, or you get life insurance and don't need it. Well, I had a half a million dollars in life insurance that would have given me two hundred thousand dollars for trauma and two years' income protection. But I cancelled it four months before being diagnosed, just because a home loan broker told me it was better to go through my Super for tax purposes.

I didn't think there would be any issues, but my Super used a sub-contractor, and they were so painful to deal with that I gave up after three months. They wanted a letter from my thyroid specialist for the issues I had during my pregnancy, and the specialist wouldn't write the letter if they didn't send her a letter explaining what they required. Nobody was willing to do what had to be done, and I was over it. That's how I missed out. I've been so upset about this, that I still have a bitter taste in my mouth. The money would have helped us so much, but like Justin always says, I have to move on…and I did.

I've created three boxes. One is for Jack, containing all his birth memories, including the diary I wrote in every day at the NICU for him, the birthday cards, his paintings and drawings, and a photo album of him growing up. I've prepared one for Elyze, too, with the same content. And finally, I've created the important box for Justin that I call the emergency box. It contains the internet passwords for all the websites we use, my personal accounts and emails with their passwords, our passports, identification documents, French paperwork, superannuation details, and Centrelink leaflets about widower help and funeral documents. I actually advise everyone to put together a box like this. If you have to flee in an emergency, you just have to take it with you. I will also add a letter explaining everything, including how I would like him to dispatch my jewellery to our children.

Preparing all this relaxes me, as I feel more in control of the situation. The "good" thing about cancer is that you can be prepared to die. Even pre-paying and arranging the details of my funeral is a good idea, because if I die in fifty years, I won't have to worry about inflation and any tax increase. It will already be paid in full. And, well, if I have to pass away soon, Justin will only have to make one phone call, and the funeral company will follow my plan. I have two appointments with two different funeral companies and will go for the cheapest. I won't be there to enjoy the party, so it's pointless to spend money on a swish coffin when we could use it for our kids' studies. Especially since I want to be cremated.

This cancer is a wakeup call for life and for a lot of things. I figure that work is the least important thing for me now, whereas I've always put my career first in the past. I wanted to get ahead and needed an intellectual challenge. Now my priorities have changed, and my family is number one, on top of my very short list. Anyway, I have the job I've always wanted: I'm the mum of a beautiful boy and a gorgeous girl. And I'd like to spend more time with them. I really hope that if I'm finally part of a clinical trial, the side-effects and treatment will allow me to continue doing so. Maybe I could start a hobby, too. I've never had one, except for salsa dancing and running when I was at business school. It would be great to do something nice for myself. Taking care of my children feels great, but it's getting more tiring as they're getting older.

My parents are about to leave. I will miss them a lot, and the kids will, too. They're so happy to have their grandparents around to play with and speak French to them. I just hope they won't be sad for too long. I can't imagine how it would be if I were gone forever. That idea breaks my heart. I really don't want to be responsible for the suffering of my children and having them grieve their mum at such a young age. That would be devastating for me. I'm supposed to be the nurturing, loving, and caring mother, the one helping them avoid pain and hardship. But even though it's in the back of my mind, returning like an uncontrollable wave, I will fight it fiercely and get better. I will destroy this stupid cancer.

My latest PET scan results show that I don't have any active tumours in my spine anymore. There are just the ones in my armpits, which are stable in size but less active than before. It's fantastic news. Overall, the pills I'm taking are improving my health. The cancer isn't gone, but I'm getting better. I'm getting more time. On the downside, the average patient will develop resistance to the treatment after eight months, and I'm already at five. My oncologist reassures me by letting me know that unlike most of her peers, she won't wait for my treatment to stop working before putting me into a trial, and the one we're thinking of is opening in three to four weeks. It's taking longer than expected due to administrative paperwork, and if it opens earlier, she will get me in there straight away. I can't wait to find out what kind of immunotherapy it is. I've read a lot about all sorts of treatments and trials, and I'm ready to find out what I will be up to. These therapies seem to be the future for cancer treatment and are producing fantastic results for those who respond.

13

Before my parents leave, Justin and I decide to enjoy some quality time and discover the wonders of the Red Centre in Uluru. I'm a bit skeptical about leaving my dad in charge of my babies, as he will have to take care of them and my mum, too. I trust him, but he's definitely not as nurturing, understanding, and patient as my sister. I ask them to call me daily to let me know how things are going, and after giving big cuddles and lots of kisses for Jack and Elyze, we leave for the airport. I'm missing my kids already.

Before leaving Sydney, I had to cut my long hair. It was down to the middle of my back, but with the kids, I always put it in a ponytail. I felt like it was suffocating me. I had to make drastic changes to my appearance if I wanted to get my positive mood back, so I cut it all off. Time for changes. I got a concave haircut, like back when I was a student at business school, ready to succeed and make the most of life. Change is always good, and it will give me back my motivation. I've regained my energy by losing my long hair. I can fly now. My next project will be losing the pregnancy weight that's been sticking to me.

I've wanted to visit the sacred rock for such a long time, and I'm glad Justin and I will see it together. As we're flying over Australia, I look out the window. There are no humans, no cables, no cities. Nothing but yellows, reds, and sometimes a bit of green. I feel so blessed to see the desert with my own eyes. All this nothingness is fascinating. I can't wait to experience the Aussie Far West.

We land in a tiny airport and take a bus to the only resort in this small town. The prices are high, and the service is poor, but who cares? We're in my dream.

The day after our arrival, we have to wake up early to catch the five-a.m. bus to King Canyon. We admire the sun rising on the desert while driving for hours across the outback. It takes us nearly three hours to get to the station, where we have a frugal breakfast. Then we jump back on the bus, and half an hour later, we're at the bottom of the canyon. After climbing about five hundred steps to arrive at the top, we walk along the edge for six kilometres. The landscape is splendid, and the weather is with us. It's not too hot with a slight breeze. The colours of the rocks are made of different concentrations of iron and provide a beautiful contrast with the green and black of the vegetation.

I feel so privileged to be here that I stop for a second to contemplate the landscape and can't help the tears that spring from my eyes. I'm still alive, and I'm here in one of the most breathtaking parts of the world. I can still walk, climb, and admire. And I'm so thankful to be able to share this special moment with my best friend and lover.

We walk down the canyon to the Garden of Eden, where we spend some time taking pictures and feeling the strength of nature in such a quiet place. A small stream gives birth to the massive water hole that's between the red walls, and I wonder where it comes from, as it looks so deserted.

We then climb back up, through a steep sort of ladder, and walk along the cliff before finishing at the canyon ring, where we started three hours earlier. It's amazing to see these rocks, shaped like piles of stones, apparently the result of the sand being moved by the waves billions of years ago. The height of the cliffs, the trees growing between massive rocks, the vegetation, and the water in such a deserted landscape, are demonstrations of the force of nature.

In such an inspirational and powerful environment, I feel small, vulnerable, like a speck of dust in an ocean of sand. My life on Earth is meaningless. I'm nothing. Or maybe just another thing dying on Earth, coming in and getting out in not even a fraction of second in the planet's life. After such a big day, a warm shower, and a quick bite, we fall asleep in no time.

On Wednesday, after a sleep-in, we walk to the centre of the resort to get our pre-booked car rental. They upgrade us, as they only have a four-wheel-drive SUV. Awesome. We drive to Uluru straight away and walk around a small part of its base for two kilometres. Every part of the sacred rock has a meaningful function for the Aboriginals. The stone is red and smoother than at the canyon. It looks like there are still some sediment deposits, but it's more like a knife painting. It's massive and impressive. I get emotional again, now that I'm finally here. I can see Uluru with my own eyes, after such a long wait. Another dream come true.

We enjoy a nice picnic before a shorter walk to a water hole. We've come after the high season, but there are still a lot of flies, always around your face, eyes, and mouth. It's the only thing I don't like here.

A thin stream leads to a sacred hole, still filled with water, so we're pretty lucky. Again, the bright red contrasts with the green of the trees and grass and the blue of the sky. We immortalise the moment with a selfie and drive back to the resort for a quick shower, so we're ready for our helicopter flight at four p.m. Justin is the co-pilot this time, while I sit at the back. The view from the sky reveals some kind of patterns: stains of high big trees surrounded by smaller bushes and circled by even smaller ones, like in the local aboriginal paintings.

In this immensity of red land and small circles of bushes, Uluru and Kata Juta rise above the ground. It's fascinating. Uluru looks like slices of red stones stacked side by side. Kata Juta is different, more like a formation of thirty-four domes, made of some red cement and pebbles. After this breath-taking trip in the air, we savour a relaxing dinner at the Pioneer Bar, the pub of the resort town, and wash down a wood-fired pizza with a refreshing beer. Again, we're in bed earlyish, as the walks, the heat, and the flies have taken the most out of us.

The next day, we drive to Kata Juta. My feet are killing me from the blisters I got from the canyon walk, so I have to do the long trek in the rock formation wearing my flip-flops. I have no choice. The back of my right heel is too painful to handle a shoe. Justin shows his support by doing the same, and we get a weird look every time we come across someone.

The view from the top of the Valley of Winds is stunning. We sit here for a while, between two gigantic domes, in the heart of the valley, looking deeply into the horizon, appreciating every detail of the scene. From here, we can view other domes, farther away, after a big drop into a luxuriant green valley and the big blue sky. The entire scenery is framed by the high wall of the red dome on each side.

Justin smokes a cigarette while I take pictures, and then it's time to go back to the car for a quick bite. There's no way I'm eating outside again with all these flies. Even in front of Uluru, they're annoying.

We finish the day on another side of Kata Juta, with a short walk between two long red domes, until we reach a lookout in the middle of a luxuriant bush. Both Uluru and Kata Juta are magical, but I have a preference for Kata Juta. More intriguing, I guess.

It's still early when we head back to the resort, so we stop by the camel farm. I didn't know there were half a million camels in Australia, more than anywhere else in the world. They're used for travel and tourism, and are also sold overseas. A good-looking one can go for millions of dollars.

After a warm shower, we finish packing and get ready for our last dinner. We take a bus to the sand dunes, where a cold beverage awaits us. An Aboriginal dance starts as we admire the sunset over Kata Juta. Once it gets dark, we walk down the dune towards a nicely set outdoor restaurant made of round tables and lit by candles. Unfortunately, there are a lot of clouds, and it's a night without stars, but we still enjoy the stories about the stars and the local tribes. At our table are an older couple from Bendigo, two mums from Sydney, and a young couple from Japan who don't understand a word we're saying, poor things. We all get to know each other, and after a bit too much alcohol, we go back to our hotel room.

The next morning, I have a ten-minute ride on a beautiful camel named Norseman. It's pretty cool, too. I only did it once before, with Laetitia when we were kids, and a circus came to the village where we used to spend our summers. We raced against each other for five minutes, without a saddle. It was fun. This time it's a much slower walk, and Justin is my official photographer.

Then, it's time to catch the plane back to Sydney. This trip was so short, and it feels like we did a lot of walking. But it's been an amazing experience, and we leave the outback dazzled. Though we're happy to have enjoyed another few days with just the two of us, it feels like we already need another holiday, just to recover from the physical effort of this one. But nope, this is the last adventure for us, at least for the time being.

My parents are leaving at the end of the week, and we won't have any more babysitters. But I can't wait to see my kids again, hold them tight in my arms, and kiss them. I'm glad to be back at home with my babies, but I can't help feeling sad that it's the end of our romantic getaways, and I don't know when it will be just the two of us again. I'm a bit scared but happy to start our new little routine, just the four of us, as a family.

14

It's Wednesday, May fourth. I have an appointment with my oncologist, and she tells me that I could start a clinical trial with Keytruda combined with a genetically modified herpes virus, but we won't know if I will actually receive the virus or a placebo in my injections. I'm excited but scared. It will be painful to get these injections. I'll have to take care of my wounds with caution, and the kids won't be able to approach me or the sensitive parts of my body.

This modified virus is supposed to indicate to my immune system the location of the tumours and get it to fight the virus right where it is. A clever trick. But even if I don't receive the virus, I will still get Keytruda either way. And if it doesn't work—which we'll know six months from now—I can go back to my current targeted therapy. So I stop my actual treatment straight away, in order to start the washout period and flush my body for the next twenty-eight days, a compulsory step before starting this trial. My spine is free of tumours now, or at least they're inactive, as any scar will always be apparent in the bones. This trial can be the next step towards my complete recovery. Or if not, it can give me more time with my loved ones and for new treatments to come.

But I'm ready. I started pre-paying for my funeral, just in case. It was painful and awkward, but I did it. I even managed to laugh about it. Justin and I wonder where he could spread my ashes and what kind of urn he will get, since these are the only decisions I left for him to sort out.

I've planned a small ceremony at the crematorium close to one of my favourite places in Sydney, La Perouse, where I'll be near the beach. It's a nice, familiar place, peaceful and dear to my heart. It's where we walked on the beach after we knew we had to say goodbye to our first baby, where I had my first ice cream dipped in chocolate and peanuts, where Jack took his first steps in the sand, and where my sister enjoyed herself when she was here. Justin will have to pick my flowers, but that's all. I'm glad he'll be able to take care of the kids and to grieve without being annoyed by all the details. It's awful to think of how my little ones will cope on that day. They won't realise what's happening and will wonder where I am. But we aren't there yet, and I have hope that I will trick my fate. I'm going to be so ready to die, that nothing will happen any time soon.

I've already started writing Elyze and Jack's birthday cards and finished the emergency box with a long letter for Justin. He will have everything he needs in case I'm not there anymore to help him out. I also started the photo book, including Elyze's birth. It's such a nice feeling to know that everything I can control has been completed.

If one day my oncologist says, "That's it. I'm sorry. There are no more options available, and you should start palliative care," I won't have to waste my precious time on all this. I'm glad it's already done. If cancer wants to kill me, I'm ready. I can now focus on surviving, enjoying my time with my family, and doing the things I love, without worrying about the *what if*.

After two weeks without treatment, the doctors attempt a biopsy on my biggest tumour and realise it's far too deep to reach, even with the longest needle they have. These technical issues mean I won't be able to go ahead with this clinical trial, but they think I can do another one that's opening up in July. I didn't like the risks of this one anyway, so maybe fate is on my side, and this small bump in the road will get me a better trial. The new one doesn't use Keytruda, but it's still an immunotherapy. I hope it's the one that will cure me. When you have cancer, all you want is to be saved from your death sentence. The hardest part of having an incurable disease is that you're not living, you're surviving. Otherwise, I would still go to work and live as usual, unaware of my potential death. I wouldn't think about the things I want to do *if* or *before* I die, or people I want to see, maybe for the last time.

That's the hardest part—uncertainty and imminent mortality. My time could come soon. I just don't know when exactly, and it's killing me. But I'm already dying anyway. It's better to laugh than cry, and my sarcastic, dark sense of humour is getting sharper as time goes by. My parents and Justin think I'm going a bit too far with the morbid jokes sometimes, but I'm trying to find some fun in the tragedy of my situation. Also, knowing that my life is in jeopardy helps me live to the fullest, and that's priceless. I just wish I could have done it without being scared of dying.

Jack is celebrating his second birthday already. He's such an awesome little dude now, talking heaps, so active and smart. He understands what's going on and that it's his birthday. He looks in every bag to see if there's a present for him. He also surprises me by grabbing a chicken kebab off the table and eating it off the stick, like we do. He's growing up so fast. When I help him blow out his candle, I make a wish that I will be able to see the wonderful man he will become.

Elyze can sit by herself and crawl. She wants to stand up all the time and loves her food. At seven months, she's nearly the size of a year-old baby. I'm so lucky to have these two in my life. They're definitely worth fighting for.

On the other hand, Justin and I are slowly drifting apart. Five years and counting, and there are no signs of romance anymore. My parents are gone, and we have no help at all. Between his labouring job and the kids, my cancer, and the financial pressure, it's hectic. We no longer have any quality time together. For most married couples, cancer brings them closer and unearths the best parts of them. It doesn't seem to be working that way for us. Two kids under three killed the romance. My husband wants to be one of these manly men and doesn't understand that nowadays, husbands need to help as much as they can with the household. He doesn't want to think that one day I may be gone, and that he will have to do all the chores and care for the kids, on top of his job. As long as he has me, he thinks he just has to go to work to fulfil his duty, and I can do all the rest of it, because I don't have a job. I'm sick of it.

I'm upset about not having any smiles and kisses in the morning. I miss the young couple days and the man I fell in love with. He used to always be happy, and the two of us would find ways to please each other. Now it's all about his remote-control cars and Xbox games. I married a teenager. I want us to behave differently towards each other, but I feel like every time I try to make things better, it's a one-way street. He doesn't want to change. For instance, his convenient smoking habit. He goes to the garage to avoid smoking in the house, but I feel he's using it as a way of avoiding us, when he takes half an hour to have a cigarette.

Though I try to focus on the good, it's difficult. He's always tired and grumpy, yelling and swearing. I don't like his attitude. I still love him, but I'm just not quite sure how long I'm going to last pretending I can deal with this turmoil. I may not have many years in front of me, and I want him to realise that. I'd like him to cherish the time we have together, with us both showing each other affection. I want more of his soft side. I'm not a soldier. I'm strong, but I'm also emotional and sensitive, and the roller coaster of emotions I've been through lately is draining our relationship. I just need for us both to be more present and loving. Sometimes I wonder if he's escaping reality by spending so much time on his phone rather than being with us. Maybe he just doesn't know how to deal with the situation. He always keeps everything to himself, while I need to talk my emotions out.

For the past five years, we've had the same argument pattern. While I attempt to understand the reasons behind our conflicts, he just switches off and leaves. I feel like he's not fighting for us. We're so different, more so than I thought. I'm outgoing, social, and driven, while he likes his solitude, doesn't trust people, and is content with his job. I love the outdoors, and he prefers staying at home. I believe in dealing with issues head on, while he prefers the silent treatment. I'm affectionate and talkative, and he's undemonstrative. But at least he listens…most of the time.

At first, all these differences didn't matter, because we worked through them and found ways to get around them. But through the years and having babies, they start to matter, especially when our support network is so weak. With less time to communicate, compromise, and understand one another, and more obstacles to overcome, it's hard for us to cope.

I feel like he's just observing his life, watching it pass by, and not being involved in any of it. It's disheartening, and at times, I even think he could be depressed, overwhelmed by the situation and denying it. It seems as if he lacks a sense of purpose, which would make him happier and more of an actor in his own life, rather than being on "auto-pilot" mode. I just want my gentleman back.

Only a month after our holidays, I feel like we need more time off already. But the reality is that we need time off from cancer. Even if it doesn't kill me, it's draining us, because it's such a crazy ride of ups, downs, bends, and U-turns. One day I'm doing great, and the next I'm in tears, sometimes for no apparent reason. But we will get through this, because at the end of the day, we still love each other, and isn't that all that matters?

Living like you're going to die any day is way too emotional for me. I can only do that for so long. I have to find some sort of routine and normalcy to stay sane. I try to enjoy every day with my young family, without having "if I die" thoughts. I'm not sure if I'll go back to work, even if I'm cured one day, as I don't earn enough to justify my entire salary going towards paying for day care, and I'd be happier having my children home with me full time. But for now, I can't physically cope with them on that level and go to doctors and other appointments. I'm trying to make decisions based on what I really want and what we can afford, rather than my condition. This way, whether I get better or not, I won't have any regrets.

I'm officially a pensioner, in a sort of retirement, trying to enjoy the few years I may have left. Like an old person, but with young babies, and definitely no one to share my spare time with. I don't have any activities to go to, and I'm desperate to find something I'm passionate about. The elitist teacher from my business preparatory class used to tell us how important it was to talk about our passions in job interviews. He said we all had to learn how to speak intelligently about them and find ways to promote ourselves through them. I didn't have any back then, and I'm still struggling to find one.

I was always into sports but never kept to one activity longer than two years. I drew a lot as a kid, but when my big sister told me I didn't have any talent, I stopped. Then I learned to dance salsa, and later, my favourite pastime was going after the guys I wanted.

But if I can't find a hobby, at least I should look for my next project. I must have something to look forward to in order to save me from insanity. I love travelling, if it can even be considered a hobby. Maybe I just need a change of scenery. I think I need to see my friends and my country again. Homesickness doesn't add up well to the equation.

I miss my sister. I'd love my kids to meet their cousins and see my family and friends. I have to find a way to bring us all to France. It would be such an awesome experience, being in my hometown with my family, catching up with my friends and my sister, watching their kids playing with mine while we chat. It's been nearly three years since I've been back, and I don't know why, but it seems to be the right amount of time for me to be homesick. The first time I went back home was also three years after I'd moved to Australia. I need to breathe the French air. I miss the French cheeses and pastries, and wonderful food in general. I just have to find a way to make such an expensive trip happen.

15

It's July fourth already. Elyze starts day care for three days a week, so I can go to my doctor appointments, get my scans, do chores, and enjoy some me time. She's nearly nine months old now and will be happier playing with her brother at day care than being trapped in the car with me. She's starting to move a lot and is getting interactive.

I'd like to find a better day care, because this one is a bit boring for them. Except for painting, they don't do any other activities, and the education isn't all that great, as they let Jack do whatever he wants. But it will stay as it is until we move into a house.

I'm glad Jack and Elyze are playing together a lot now. Elyze is so intrigued by her brother, and he doesn't wrestle her anymore, because he's probably figured out she's also a human being. They love to play hide and seek. She's eating well and taking the spoon out of my hands to do it herself. She's such a little woman already, getting her independence quickly and caring for all of us with her sweet and cuddly attitude. She's a real little Frenchy, loving bread and cheese. She said *"Maman"* clearly two days ago. Justin and I looked at each other with a smile. It wasn't the usual babbling. It means "Mum" in French. And since then, she hasn't stopped. Jack is starting to get a bit jealous of all the attention she's getting and is asking to be held a lot lately

Justin feels a bit left out, because he thinks they're both mama's kids. I'm sure he'll soon be fed up when they start asking for more of his time. But I'm a bit worried that Elyze hasn't bonded much with him. I've been the one taking care of her since birth. Justin has only given her a bath a few times and never puts her to bed at night or wakes up for her. He should do it more often. It's important for them to bond.

Also, I can't wait for the kids to have their own bedrooms. It's so tough putting them to bed. Jack makes bedtime painful. We've visited several houses for rent, but nothing seemed to be right for us—either too expensive or not good enough—until we see an ad for a lovely three-bedroom house in Blakehurst. It's quite far from where we live, and there's no train station around, but when we get there, we both agree it's perfect.

Old but big, it has three bedrooms and a bathroom with a bath and shower. This means the kids can still have their bath time together. It has a lovely backyard, a big family room, a formal lounge room, a large kitchen with potential for a dishwasher, and a garage converted into a workshop for Justin. Okay, we can't buy a house in crazy-expensive Sydney, but we can rent. We just have to wait for the landlord to get back to us.

I hope we'll get it, because it would be a great relief not only to have the kids in separate rooms, but the big rumpus could be a great playroom for them, surrounded by windows, and we all won't feel so claustrophobic anymore. I could live again in this place. I don't even wait for their answer to start packing. We've accumulated so much stuff since the two bags that started our life together. The potential move-in is in two weeks, and I want to be prepared.

Having a few days a week for myself allows me to start organising our trip to France. I started a fundraiser to finance it. Going back home for Christmas would be amazing. I love the holiday season. I miss a cold Christmas and the charming French markets. Also, I can't think of a better present than seeing my family again and introducing my babies to my aunties, cousins, nephews, and friends.

I'm not the kind of person to ask for help, and even less so in regards to money, but times are tough, and it would mean the world to me to celebrate my first Christmas back home since I left. The only fundraiser I've ever done was for the Melanoma March back in December, and it was quite a success. But this time, my former workmates, friends, and family are all in. They've been so generous and are glad to help us spend Christmas together. I'm moved by their kindness, and I'm again astonished by how Australians are always so keen to help their community members.

I asked for a Christmas miracle, and they made it happen. We raise enough to buy four tickets to Paris in order to spend Christmas with my family. I'm ecstatic for Jack and Elyze to be able to meet their cousins and the rest of their family for the first time. We'll spend a cold, and hopefully white, Christmas in France. I'm so proud to introduce my young family to everyone. It feels good, looking forward to such a tremendous event. I miss my roots. Even if I was happy to leave, it represents my childhood, and it's calling for me. I long to be there.

I can't go back without organising something with my best friends, Gilda, Aurélie, and Laure. I met them in business school thirteen years ago, and we never lost contact. Every time we catch up, it's like we've spent no time apart. Seven years feels like a lifetime.

Gilda is still single, but Aurélie is married to Fabio, an Italian who seduced her during one of their company's night events. They have a five-year-old son, Antoine. Laure is married too, and living in her hometown of Bordeaux with her husband, Stéphane, and their two kids, Margaux, four and a half, and Gabriel, ten months old. We decide to spend New Year's Eve together at Aurélie's new house, hoping that the renovation will be finished by then. I couldn't be happier. It's going to be so awesome for me, the kids, and even for Justin, as they all speak excellent English, not like the rest of the Frenchies we're going to catch up with during this trip.

I'm so excited. It's such an amazing time to look forward to. Maybe we can even stop by Sainte Tulle on our way to Montpellier, to have a quick bite with my parents and family friends, Gisèle and Gilbert. I've known them since birth, and they're family to me. But we will definitely stay one night in Montpellier with my Aunty Françoise and Uncle Michel before spending New Year's Eve weekend with the girls. Back home, a two-hour drive is pretty much a day trip, while you can drive the same amount of time in Australia, just for a return trip to your favourite coffee shop. When I lived in France, if I'd perceived distance the way I do now, I would have travelled so much more.

As the numbers get higher on the fundraising page, one of my former workmates suggests squeezing in my dream of going to New York. At first, I think it's crazy, since travelling to Europe with two kids under the age of three will be hard enough, especially with the jet lag and all. But then I think, *Why not? When will I get a chance to do it again? We only live once, right?* So I check flight prices with my travel agent, and we find the cheapest round-the-world tickets. There will be a lot of stops and planes, but we can stay in New York City for three days. It will be freezing there, too, but I've wanted to go to New York since Mum told me she went there with a wealthy Portuguese family she nannied for when she was a student. I was a child back then, but I still remember the black-and-white photo of my mum in front of the crazy-high building and the feeling of freedom and happiness she experienced when she told me her story. It seemed like she had the time of her life there, and I want to experience the same feeling. Under the snow would be even better.

Soon I'll be able to tick the box of travelling the world, as we will actually go around the planet: Sydney – Hong Kong – Frankfurt – Paris – Nice – Zurich – New York – Los Angeles – Sydney. Okay, it sounds crazy to do that with two babies, but I can't wait to live this big adventure with my family. I'm so thankful to all the people who've helped make my dreams become a reality.

My oncologist confirms that I can be a part of the upcoming trial. It will be two immunotherapies combined: Keytruda and another one, in a tablet this time. I hope it will work for me…after all, it can be the cure of tomorrow. If I'm accepted for this trial, I will have to receive the infusion of Keytruda the day we leave and on the day we come back, so I book our flights accordingly. These infusions must be done every three weeks, so we can only stay five days total in Nice and three days in Montpellier, before leaving for New York. It will be a lot of moving, but we have no choice. I just hope I won't be too exhausted, as I'm already tired just thinking of this hectic holiday. I guess it's a small price to pay to go around the world and tick three items off my bucket list.

Another dream came true on July 22, 2016. We got our approval and have just moved into the Blakehurst house. I'm over the moon. Everything is coming together for us, and I couldn't be happier. I finish unpacking in two days. Justin thinks I'm crazy, as I don't stop for a minute, but I hate living out of boxes, and I'm glad to have everything in order and see how nice the house is. It's so big. We need more furniture, so I find a great deal on Gumtree. A nice bloke from Manly is getting rid of two beautiful brown leather lounges and a coffee table for free on that exact weekend, as he's moving and couldn't find a buyer. Perfect timing.

Justin picks them up, and they fit seamlessly in front of the fireplace, in our formal lounge room. I place our big family portrait canvas on top of the fireplace, and it becomes my favourite spot in the house. The kids have their massive playroom, and they love it. I sleep so well here. I usually snooze in the afternoon while Elyze naps for two or three hours. She's definitely a great baby, even though she now wakes up at night, because she's teething. Jack is still clingy and doesn't want to share me with his sister, so he's full of tantrums. But he's so good at putting himself to bed now. We just have to leave him with a light on and a book, and he eventually falls asleep. It's so much better for all of us, not having to pat him forever.

But between taking care of the kids and all the packing and unpacking, I'm exhausted and don't have much chance to do anything for myself since Elyze started day care. It's lucky that Justin and I have an extra hour for some quality time together every night, since we now have a dishwasher, my new favourite machine. I'm so happy in this house, I don't want to go outside anymore. It's so bright with all these big windows everywhere. It's not our house, but it feels like home, and that's all that matters.

To tick another box, I started a diet with prepared meals, giving me only twelve-hundred calories a day, and I'm exercising again. I had to lose the pregnancy weight to feel better in my skin, and I did. Plus, exercising gives me some energy back. I'm not training like the madwoman I used to be, but doing an hour of light cardio with abs and butt toning daily helps me feel better about myself. I've gone from sixty-three kilos to fifty-six, in six weeks. I can fit into my clothes again, and that in itself is an amazing feeling. I'm back to a size ten and can even fit into my old jeans, so I've thrown out all the size fourteen clothes I bought after my pregnancy. I have my young body back. Everything seems possible now, and I don't need anything else. I have the house, the lighter body, the trip to France to see my loved ones, and even New York. I just need a clean bill of health, and then I'll actually believe in miracles.

16

It's August 5, 2016, and I'm thirty-five today. It seems like I've lived a lifetime, because I've already accomplished so much.

Since being diagnosed, I've had lots of flashbacks of my life. My friends, parties, studies, boyfriends, family…moments that seemed insignificant at the time, but I can recall so vividly. There are a lot of "If I'd done things differently," or "if I die." Apparently, when you're about to leave the planet, you see all the images of your life before your last breath. I feel like that's what's happening, but in slow motion. Where would I be if I'd slightly changed some moments of my past? But I can't think like that. I can only live in the now, and that's okay. I wouldn't change a thing, even all the stupid mistakes I've made, because they brought me where I am today, and it's where I want to be. Thinking about all the "what ifs" helps me realise that if I had to die now, I would have no regrets.

I never suspected I would live in another country, speak a different language, and be so far away from everything I'd ever known. My past experiences, good or bad, have made me the person I've become. I don't want to be anywhere else, with anybody other than Justin. I love my husband, even if he can be annoying, grumpy and undemonstrative at times, and since day one, wouldn't dress the way I like. He's kind, generous, and such a funny soul when he wants to be. The most genuine, too. He gave me the most beautiful presents ever: two amazing kids. They're my pride and joy, and the best thing I've ever done in my life. They're my world.

I've survived thirty-five years so far, and I want at least another thirty-five. I have terminal cancer, and I'm the happiest woman on Earth. But the happier I get, the more scared I become. Because the more I have, the more I have to lose, and I don't want to lose any of it. I've worked too hard for all of this, I've sacrificed so much and had so many years of sadness and struggles. It feels like I've just started being happy. I don't want this birthday to be the last one. Birthdays are like Christmases; they raise so many emotions. They make you think back on all you've achieved so far, the people you love, the things you look forward to, and where you are now. And I'm happy where I am, so I just have to focus on that and leave the fear aside.

Ten days after my birthday, I stop my treatment, so I can begin the clinical trial. Once again, it's not the one I'd originally planned for, because it's been delayed, but an open spot came up for another one. When my oncologist offered it to me. I jumped on it, because who knows when the other trial will finally open? I've been waiting months. Also, this one gives me the opportunity to access a drug that's not yet been approved. The original clinical trial was composed of Keytruda, which is already approved and available to me if my actual treatment fails, along with a protein called IDO that tells the immune system which cells to fight by revealing the hidden cancer cells. But I'd only have a one in two chance of getting the protein, as it's a randomised trial. With this new trial, I can get an anti-PDL1, which in theory should work as efficiently as Keytruda, and a protein called CD137 that boosts the immune system by increasing the number of T-cells to fight the cancer. I would get the combination for sure, as there's no randomisation for this one.

It will be intense, with an infusion of Anti-PDL1 every two weeks and one of CD137 every four weeks. The infusion itself will last an hour, and I will have to stay another couple of hours afterward to make sure I'm fine. I also have to come to the Melanoma Institute every week for an entire day in order to go through some tests. This trial has been given to patients with other cancers, too, with great results so far. Only seven people will be chosen from Australia, out of the twenty-eight melanoma patients around the world, as well as eighteen other cancer patients. I feel so lucky to be considered and hope to be accepted this time. It's my third attempt for a trial so far. I have to stop my treatment for twenty-eight days to flush my body again, so we should be able to see the results from the trial within four months. I hope it will work, because stopping my treatment for five months could be dangerous.

I can always go back to my treatment afterward if it doesn't work. Justin tells me he would do the same and trusts my judgment anyway. He's so tired lately. Without my parents' help and with lack of sleep, we're both burnt out. The kids are draining all our energy. Elyze is waking up at night, with four teeth coming in at the same time, and she's been sick quite often since she started day care. Jack is still clingy, and I don't know what's wrong. Sometimes I think he knows that my life is threatened and tries to stay with me as much as he can.

The good news is that I'm seven kilos down. I've revised my goal to fifty-four, as this diet is driving me nuts. It's great but hard not getting my chocolate treats. If I have to die, I want to be able to indulge a bit, too. I just have to be reasonable. Also, I've been a bit slack with cooking dinners for Justin and the kids, and it's getting costly to continue these diet meals anyway. I dropped all the pregnancy weight, so it's all about maintenance now.

A day later, I have my first PET scan in four months. I think my cancer is still stable, as I haven't felt anything wrong except for some side-effects of my treatment. I see my oncologist the next Monday. I'm nervous, because I've been on my treatment for nine months, and she'd told me people become resistant around eight. I'm hopeful for some good news.

"So I have some good and bad news," she says as I sit down in her office. "The good news is that the PET scan revealed no evidence of disease (NED). It means that the tumours may still be present, but they're not active."

"Wow, so that's great. I mean, it's what every cancer patient wants to hear, right?"

"Yes, that's fantastic. But the bad news is that because there's only one tumour at three millimetres showing on the scan, it's too small for you to be accepted for the trial."

"What can we do now?"

"We don't know how long this situation can last, especially since you're not on any treatment right now. So what we can do, if you agree, is that you'll stay off treatment for another three weeks, and we'll see if the tumours get bigger."

"Okay. As long as it's not too dangerous for me," I reply, a bit concerned.

"It's great news that you've responded so well to your treatment, but we have to try immunotherapy, because it works better early in the diagnosis."

"But if it doesn't work, I can still go back to my combo treatment, right?"

"Yes."

"It's been nine months. Do you think I could become resistant?"

"Well, that's only a statistic. Also, you could be part of the 10 to 15 percent of people who never become resistant.

"Has losing the extra weight helped?"

"Being healthy and eating well may have helped in clearing the tumours. But don't worry. We'll do another scan in three weeks, and I'll see you after. And remember, being NED is great news."

I'm a bit scared to bring the cancer back for the purpose of these trials. I hope immunotherapy will work as good as my treatment, if not better. If it does, my immune system will apparently recall how to fight, so I'll be able to stop the treatment at some point and still get the benefits from it.

With each passing day, the great news transforms into anxiety. It's so hard for me to deal with the chance of this cancer coming back anywhere, especially in the brain, which is my biggest fear. But I also wonder if I could stay NED long enough to go back to a "normal" life. The uncertainty of what's going to happen, and the question of what I should do with my life if I survive, worries me. I love taking care of my kids and having more time for them and myself. I won't have that precious time if I go back to work full time.

Just thinking about working again with my previous careless boss gives me panic attacks. He never asked if I was doing well, donated to any of my fundraisers, sent a text to check if I was coming back at any point, or even if I was alive. I don't really want to have to deal with him anymore. That's the thing when your life is at stake—you want to use your time mindfully, with worthy people.

There's not enough time to waste anymore. Every second counts. Even queuing at the shop is annoying, and spending an hour in a traffic jam is excruciating. Time becomes the most valuable commodity in your world, so you choose carefully what you want to do with it, even if you squander some of it creating a photo book or watching TV. I may have to look for another job not too far from home, as I don't want to spend hours driving when I can be with my kids. Also, I'm thinking of working for a company that does good for the planet and for its people, Maybe I can get a part-time job, so I can stay with my kids one or two days a week, at least until they go to school. Anyway, I have to make sure I can remain stable for a while before jumping the gun. But for now, I need to concentrate on starting a trial.

All this anxiety weighs on me, and soon Justin and I reach the breaking point. We need some time off, so he plans for his brother to keep the kids for once, but Jay cancels at the last minute. It's one drop too many in my already overflowing cup. We need time together, and we can't find any. Between my health, uncertainty about work, money issues, and all the rest of it, I've had enough. I'm pissed off because I don't understand why people don't keep their word. So that afternoon, I take off after another argument. This time he's not the one who leaves, I am. It feels good, but I'm driving without knowing where to go.

I could get a coffee to calm myself down, but instead, I decide to go to the movies to watch *Bad Moms*. I couldn't have found a better movie for the occasion. I laugh so hard and realise that I'm asking way too much of myself and can't go on like this. I have to take it easy and learn to let go. Be less of a perfectionist. It's already hard enough to cope with terminal cancer and two babies, so being the perfect housewife will have to wait. I need to do less, or at least less often, and find more time for myself and to be with Justin, even if we have to trust his dad to babysit. It would only be a couple of hours, anyway. I have to be kind to myself. Overdoing it is how I stay away from thinking too much, but I have to stop, or it will kill me, my marriage, or both.

It's time to enjoy my new body and my new home, and try to relax. But for me, duties have always come first, and pleasure occurs only if you still have time for it. The thing is that nowadays, if you don't plan time for doing what you love, you will never have a chance to relax. There's always something to do. When I come back home on time to help Justin feed the kids and prepare them for bed, I enter the house with a smile and thank my husband for the afternoon I had for myself before pouring a glass of wine. Dinners usually stress me out, because Jack never wants to eat, and as his weight gain has always been an issue, I never stop worrying about it. But tonight, I don't force the issue, and everything works out fine.

I also figure that I have to socialise. Back home, I used to be such a social butterfly, but my backpacker friends are all long gone now, so I reach out to the melanoma community on social media and ask if there are any mums out there, close to my place, who would like to catch up some time. That's how I meet Kerry, another stage four melanoma patient and mum of three young teenagers.

It's the first week of October 2016, nearly a year after my diagnosis, when we decide to go for a coffee at Carss Park, which is next door to my place. During our first meeting, we talk for nearly four hours. It feels so good to meet another mum with the same condition. I've finally found someone who gets me. Someone who can understand what I'm going through and doesn't judge me but supports me. I can be myself with her, with all my fears and morbid sense of humour. She's going through the same stuff and becomes a sort of melanoma sister. I also become friends with three other stage four mums on Facebook.

Justin and I spend the long weekend of our fifth wedding anniversary at home potty training Jack. I keep him home another three days to make sure we're on the right track before returning him to day care. He's been doing great, with only one or two accidents since. I'm so proud of him. My baby is becoming a little boy.

Elyze is about to celebrate her first birthday, and I can't help but feel emotional again. When her big day arrives, I prepare a great party for her. I clean the house all week and bake two chocolate cakes, one for day care and one for the evening at home. She's super excited both times and rushes to eat them. She's so happy to see the candle and hear us sing the Happy Birthday song for her. She even tries to grab the lollies I placed on top of the cake. Jack and I help her blow out the candle, while dad films the scene. It's perfect. She's perfect. She even manages to rip all the paper to open her presents. I can't believe she's one already.

I couldn't have asked for better babies. Jack's clinginess and Elyze waking us up with her teething are small issues. I'm so grateful for my healthy children. They're magnificent, smart, alert, expressive, and affectionate. I love them more than myself. Their life will always come before mine. If I had to go through cancer to have my beautiful Elyze, then it was worth it. I love her and Jack with all my heart and soul. Before becoming a mum, I didn't know what unconditional love was, but now I do. It's the most beautiful feeling anyone can ever experience, being so deeply linked to another human being. They are my blood, my guts.

I always knew I wanted to be a mother from the first time I played with dolls. But I didn't know how good it would feel. It's so rewarding, inspiring, and surprising, even if it can also be painful and difficult at times. My kids smiling and laughing, running towards me when I pick them up at day care, feeling their little bodies against me when they give me a cuddle, and hearing Jack say, *"Je t'aime maman"* ("I love you, Mama" in French), are the most precious moments ever.

I'm so thankful to have met Justin. Like any couple, we're going through ups and downs, even more so when circumstances create such hardships. But through it all we still love each other, and I'm so glad he gave me the chance to be a mum. I just hope I'm good at it, because I'm trying my best. I feel at home anywhere with these three. And I can't wait to be with all the other people I love, back in my country of birth, to show them off.

The PET scan from November shows that I'm still stable, so there's no growth and no activity. This means I won't be doing the trial but also that my worries and the weird feeling in my left armpit, as well as the pins and needles, were probably just the normal weird stuff. It's hard not to worry when you don't have any safety net. I'm climbing a cliff with no cord, just my arms holding me suspended on the edge, and I can fall at any time. It's difficult to live like this, and it requires so much strength that I feel like I can barely breathe at times. It's tiring.

I'm angry at the system. I don't understand how governments can put millions into war equipment and weapons research, when people still die of cancer. Or that we still haven't found a cure, when we're able to go to Mars. Yet, I am thankful I'm still alive and in a good shape. I feel lucky when my oncologist tells me that it's rare after three months of no treatment not to have any reoccurrence. So I'm happy to win more time and defy the odds, even if I'm a bit anxious.

I've always been the anxious kind. I got that from my mum and dad, who are both perfectionists. But these days, I've really begun to understand the extent of it: difficulty sleeping, over-thinking, feeling tense all the time, and being edgy and short. I hate it, but I'm trying hard to cope, and meditation is the best thing I've done to help me live with it and make it bearable. Also, I think that being okay with no treatment is pretty sweet, and it won't happen often, so I have to enjoy it while it lasts. I can pretend to be normal and healthy for now, and that's priceless. I try to make the most out of it by exercising every day and enjoying life as much as I can. The glass is half full, and I hope it will stay that way.

One good thing about not doing the trial is that I can increase the length of my stay in France. I change my flight tickets, so we can have ten more days in Paris. We'll leave Sydney on the eleventh of December and stay in Paris until the twenty-seventh. This way we'll be able to recover from jet lag and have more time with my sister and her kids. Then Mum and Dad will join us on the seventeenth. We'll stay for ten days in a flat close to my sister's place in Villejuif, a suburb outside Paris, because it's too tiny for the five of them, much less adding us to the mix. So we'll all spend Christmas Eve together and Christmas day at my aunty Solange's with her husband and three kids.

I'm a bit concerned for Jack, as he wakes up at night screaming like crazy and has stopped gaining weight again, so the paediatrician put him back on the reflux medicine. I think he has sleep apnoea, and she advised me to do a sleep study, but we'll have to wait until March to see a physician. His tonsils are so big. He's snoring at night and sweaty. Most of the time he ends his nights in our bed. I can hear him stop breathing at times, and he usually freaks out. I'm hoping he'll be okay until then, but I'm upset we have to wait so long. Since he was eight months old, he's struggled to grow, and Elyze is as tall as he is now. His weight chart looks like a staircase. I want my boy to thrive and to stop worrying. I'm upset the doctors have to wait so long to treat him, just because we don't have any private health insurance. Why can't we remove these tonsils if they're the cause of his sleeping issues? It's obvious that it could also be the reason why he's not growing properly, on top of the reflux. Poor thing. I feel guilty again, having given birth too early, but I have to let it go. I'm doing the best I can to find out what's going on. I just need to be patient and know that we'll deal with it when the time comes.

17

Before our trip to France, I get my last scan results and am unbelievably still stable. I'm scheduled to have another PET and CT scan when we return to Sydney, but for now, it's holiday time. I'm exhausted already. Being a full-time mum of a toddler and a baby is hard work, but I'd wanted to figure out if I was able to do it, and was desperate to spend more time with them, so I took them off day care a month ago. It was great the first week, but it's been harder and harder as time goes on. I haven't had a minute to rest or just to wee by myself. And yet, I enjoy every minute of it. When we get back, I'll return to using day care once or twice a week, so I can do the chores and have actual quality time with them on the days they're home. We spend most of our time playing, going to the park, or shopping, the last being super painful with both of them.

It's been hard on our marriage, too. I asked Justin for more help in the evenings, but I would rather have him stay away than whining while helping me.

I found a great day care for the kids to start in mid-January, and Justin will take a week off after our big trip to recover from the holiday. Sometimes, I just want to have a nice chat with him while drinking a beer at the pub or going for a coffee, but it feels like we don't know how to spend quality time together anymore. Maybe I can ask my mum and dad to keep the kids one night while we have some well-deserved time off.

We arrive in Paris after three planes and two airport transfers. The one in Hong Kong was awesome. They had these little capsules on wheels, so we placed Jack and Elyze in two of them and raced down the extra-long corridor that led us to the train used to transport us to the other side of a town-sized terminal. Jack loved the plane but slept very little, maybe seven hours out of thirty-five. He watched a lot of cartoons on the onboard entertainment screen, though. Elyze could only sleep attached to me in the baby carrier, so I spent the whole time sitting with twelve kilos of baby over me.

After spending three days recovering from the plane trip, we enjoy a day in Paris, walking down one of my favourite streets, *Rue Mouffetard*, and eating crepes for lunch. The kids actually love the French food. I don't have to worry at all about Jack. I've never seen him eat like this.

Then we go through the Pantheon to reach the Luxembourg gardens. The immense park has a big playground for the kids, and we spend a couple of hours playing there. After that, we take the bus to return home, and Jack loves it. He's looking at the people walking on the street and makes friends with some old people sitting next to him. It's the kids' first time on a bus, as we always take the car in Sydney. It was also their first time on a plane, so there's been lots of excitement for Jack within just a few days.

Since we arrived in France, we've indulged ourselves with a baguette with jam or *pain au chocolat* and croissants for breakfast every morning. Each time I come back, I remember how good the food is. Everything tastes so much better, and shopping for fruits, veggies, cheeses, and breads is much cheaper than in Sydney. Also I wish we had as many frozen choices. There's even a retail shop that specialises in frozen food.

Everybody works late, so they have lots of ready-to-cook meals, and at a cheap price tag, too. This is awesome for the working mum and time-poor families. The traceability of any kind of food is a legal requirement, so we always know where the product comes from, which is definitely something I would like to have in Sydney. I'd say Australia is great for a lot of things but behind for others, like food legislation and medical care accessibility for kids. A child shouldn't be a public or private patient; they should always be taken care of as quickly as possible, whatever their parent's financial situation.

After five days, the kids start to recover from jet lag, so it's lucky we arrived earlier. I don't think it would have been good if they hadn't recovered by the time the Christmas festivities began. I'm so glad to be here for my sister's children's birthday. The twins are two years old already. She came over a few nights ago with my four-year-old niece, Emy, but this is the first time the five cousins are together. Elyze walks around happy, while Jack looks like a tiny prawn compared to the twins. They're seven months younger than he is, and so big and strong. I want Jack to grow and catch up. But otherwise, he's talking a lot and is alert for his age.

It's a bit crowded and hectic in the small lounge room, but it's great to finally see them playing together. After all this time, my sister and I are getting what we've always wanted. Elyze is calm, and Jack, even though he's excited, behaves without any fuss. They seem like angels compared to their cousins. I feel for my poor sister, as she takes care of her kids by herself most nights, because her partner comes home from work long after their bedtime. They're struggling in their cramped flat, which makes me feel even luckier to have a house with plenty of space.

Justin is tired and not used to being with our children full time. He's short and edgy. I can't wait to have some quality time with him and get some help from my parents. My head has been spinning since we landed, and I'm overtired. The flat my dad found for us isn't kid-friendly. It has stairs and floor tiles, and Jack and Elyze hurt themselves all the time. We have to pay attention constantly, which is even more exhausting.

But it gets worse when Mum and Dad finally arrive, because nobody has any privacy. Everyone's living on top of each other, so we try to be out and about as often as possible in order to breathe. It's cold, and just dressing up both children with all their layers of clothes takes us an hour, but it's nice to go around Paris or to my sister's. I've missed France, the food, the familiar feeling of knowing the products and brands, the streets, speaking French all the time, and watching French TV, too.

It's weird. I had some trouble re-adapting myself during the first week, but now it's like I've never left. I'm a bit overwhelmed with the planning of Christmas and living with my parents again. They're definitely getting old; not just physically, but mentally. Mum can't stand the kids screaming and crying. They both have their little habits, and it's hard for all of us to live together that way. But we still enjoy some tourist time together and go to the Christmas markets on the *Champs Elysées*.

The kids play in the magic forest, and I'm glad to see the Christmas decorations on the beautiful avenue. Later in the afternoon, my parents go back home while we walk to the *Galleries Lafayette* and *Le Printemps* to admire the animated displays they create every year for Christmas. The shop windows are decorated with paper artwork, handmade and articulated bears and penguins, wheels, and castles. Jack and Elyze enjoy looking at the displays, listening to the music, and staring at all the lights. A few days later, we see "the big tower," as Jack likes to call the Eiffel Tower. Once my parents leave and the kids are asleep, Justin and I have a nice romantic walk along the Seine. It's good to feel the Christmas spirit in the cold air.

We celebrate Christmas Eve at Laetitia's, and it starts an endless flow of reunions. I'm happy to be here with my twin sister, her partner, and their children, as well as my parents and extended family. Our kids all play together, finally, after all these years dreaming about it. Though she didn't come, my older sister, Julie had left presents for my dad to give to all the children, and I'm saddened when I see there aren't any for mine. Julie and I have a broken relationship. She's barely talked to me since I was fifteen, though I've tried reaching out to her through the years. There was some communication after I was diagnosed, but even then she thought it was hypocritical for us to talk to each other, just because I was sick. But I don't care. I want my big sister back.

We see about sixty of my favourite people in the same week. Christmas day is awesome at my Aunty Solange's in Arcueil, another suburb of Paris. There are twenty-three people in all, good food and wine, many kids playing together, and lots of chatting about everything, including Australia. It's been over fifteen years since I've seen my cousins, when my Grandma Denise passed away, yet it feels like I just saw them last week. It's such a warm feeling to be with them and finally meet their children.

The next day is our last in Paris. When we come back from my aunty's, I decide to finish packing, so we can leave early in the morning and enjoy the time we have left. While taking our clothes out of the wardrobe, I see some presents on the top shelf and realise they're from my sister, Julie. Dad must have forgotten to bring them to the party. While I'm glad to realise she did acknowledge my children for the first time, I'm disappointed in my dad for forgetting them, because he should have known how much it would mean to see my children opening the presents with their cousins.

Overwhelmed by the holiday and my emotions, I start arguing with my parents about how they forgot the presents. But afterwards I also experience one of the best moments I've ever had with my daughter. After getting this off my chest, I decide to calm down by sitting on the floor and playing with her, despite the tears rolling down my cheeks, when a small miracle happens.

Elyze crawls towards me, takes me in her arms, and gives me her first kiss. It's so sweet. I'm shocked and stunned by the empathy she shows for a little girl only a few months old. I smile as I look into her eyes, my hands around her shoulders, and kiss her back.

"Thank you, you're beautiful," I say. "I love you so much, my Bubbles." We gave Elyze this nickname, because since she was only a few weeks old, she's made bubbles with her mouth. I'm stunned she can understand how sad I am and finds a way to make me feel better. This moment of peace, and noticing how my babies can be affected by my mood swings, is what I need to make me stop and calm down. I'm lucky to have them by my side on this awful journey. They're the light at the end of the tunnel, my positive thoughts and the source of my strength and resilience. I believe in the power of love, and my love for my children will save me. I will defy the odds for them. Nothing is impossible for me to stay here for them.

After the argument, Justin and I decide to find a hotel in Nice. While I've calmed down and understood my dad certainly meant no harm when he forgot the presents, and I've apologised, after living on top of each other, out of our routines, and in a not at all kid-friendly tiny space, we figured it would be a good idea for all of us to separate.

I ask for a break, hoping they won't take it personally. They've also been sick, and it's better for all of us to be apart for the next three days, so they can recover without sharing their germs with the children. And besides, we'll be back again together for our last week in France. We all need some time off. Family is great, but it's tough spending two weeks stuck together in a shoe box. The most important thing is to spend quality time together.

Overall, Paris has been nice, but not as good as when we went three years earlier. With the cold, two babies, and a pram, it's hard to move around and enjoy some romance.

18

On the twenty-seventh of December, we fly to Nice. It's a painful day for us. Security check is a nightmare. We're without prams, so I'm holding the kids in my arms, and all the baby food is checked more carefully than for the last three international flights we've taken so far. Also, the crew places Jack by himself in the aircraft during check-in, so we have to be moved around for Justin to be able to sit with him. Plus, our hand luggage doesn't fit in the overhead lockers. Then, after an hour-delayed landing, we have to wait nearly two hours queuing for our car rental. The only good thing is that we've been upgraded, otherwise our luggage and baby seats wouldn't have fit in the car.

When we arrive in the city, we manage to park after two hours of driving around the block, and walk back to the hotel through the pedestrian street of the city centre. We deserve a break, so we stop for a bite and some margaritas to relax from this hectic day. It's nice to be seated outside, watching the people and finally have a relaxing hour. We even meet one of my friends as she's passing by with her mates. We're definitely merrier when we leave to check in our hotel.

We spend our first morning going to Old Nice, my favourite area. Justin is already better, as it's warmer, so he can wear only his T-shirt.

I've missed the micro-climate of my hometown and its three hundred days of sun a year.

After a quick walk through the *Cours Saleya* market, we go for lunch on *Place de la République*, at a restaurant where five of my school friends are waiting for us with their partners and kids. We have an awesome time and stay all afternoon chatting about everything and anything, like we just talked yesterday.

We even have a conversation about my cancer. With them, it's easy and honest, not judgemental or pitiful. It's nice to be able to discuss the subject with no dramatization, no taboo, no precautions, just being myself, and they're genuinely concerned without overdoing it. It's a nice refreshing change, and I appreciate their friendship.

I realise how much I miss laughing and talking to them. They all have their own character traits and way of interacting with me. I'm also happy to meet their kids for the first time and show off mine. It's like we're back in our school days. We haven't changed much physically, but now most of us have kids, and it's funny to see us as parents.

After a nice long lunch, we walk back to the hotel through the pedestrian alley the city built a couple of years ago. It's such a beautiful city centre now, with gardens, playgrounds, and a large fountain made of enlightened water sprays coming from the ground and reflecting everything like we're walking on a lake. It's been a wonderful day, and Justin and I are happy again. The hotel room is spacious and cosy, and the blinds help us with a long sleep-in. The kids don't even wake up before ten a.m.

The next morning, we're on laundromat duty for three hours, just before joining my cousin Laurent, his daughter Lilly, and my cousin Sophie, at *Place Masséna*, in the city centre, two minutes away from our hotel. We have some *niçoises* specialties in Old Nice for lunch and go for a coffee before catching up with my big sister, Julie, her husband,

Olivier, and their eleven-year-daughter, Noémie. It's weird to see my sister. She wouldn't meet with us last time we were in France. It's been seven years since I've seen her, and double as many years since we've had a proper chat together.

Noémie is so choked up to see us. Julie didn't tell her we would be there, as she wanted to surprise her. Well done. Noémie is nearly in tears. She's as tall as I am now and so grown up. She's excited to play with the kids, so we all walk to the playground. Julie doesn't talk to me but spends her time playing with Jack and talking to Justin. Elyze is sticking to me and doesn't want any part of my family. I'm glad my sister came, even if we don't chat. After years of not talking, it's awkward for me too, I don't know what to say, either, so I'm just happy to take her in my arms and somehow make peace.

My niece is happy to chat with me and loves her cousins. Lilly, my cousin Laurent's daughter, didn't really speak with Jack and Elyze. Her mother is English, so she can understand them, but speaking it is another story. I hope Elyze and Jack will be able to have a conversation in French one day, so they can all stay in touch. It will be hard for them to grow up without their cousins.

We leave Nice the next day for Montpellier and stop by Sainte Tulle to have lunch with Gisèle and Gilbert, our family friends and godparents of my big sister. They're happy to meet the kids and see me. The cancer talk, again, is like with the rest of the family; a bit guarded. But still, it's nice to be able to speak freely about it. And of course, they're hoping I will stay clear forever. It's weird that I feel upset every time someone says that. It's as if they're quickly dismissing the fact that my condition is terminal and this thing may catch me one day for good.

Of course, I hope they're right, but the feeling I get is that they're trying to comfort or protect themselves and believe they're protecting me as well. I'm still struggling to accept the various ways people deal with my condition, but I understand how difficult it must be for them to know the right thing to say to me. Every person might take things differently, and it's hard to figure how to express yourself in tragic circumstances.

We arrive at my auntie's in the evening. Françoise, Michel, and my cousin, Adrien, welcome us home, and it's good to see them again. I studied in this city and used to see them often back then. Françoise is the youngest of my mum's sisters, and she and Michel are so down to Earth. It's good to see all of these people who were such a big part of my life growing up.

I tell them how glad I am to see them after catching up with their son and brother, Olivier, back in Paris. By now, I've pretty much seen my entire family: my parents, my two sisters, my two aunties, their husbands, all my cousins except for one, and all of their kids. I will see my Uncle Gérard back in Nice in a couple of days. Sometimes these reunions make me feel uncomfortable. Because while these people I love are doing their thing, and I try to enjoy every moment with them, capturing their faces and laughter in my mind and experiencing it all at maximum intensity, I feel they're living it on a much shallower level, the way I used to.

The next morning, we go for a walk with Françoise and Adrien in the historic city centre, and I'm happy to show Justin and the kids where I lived for two years. I've missed all these historic old towns. I admire the old streets paved with stones and the sandstone medieval buildings. We have a last yummy meal with them before leaving for Cabrières, a small village in the countryside, where we will spend New Year's Eve with my best friends from business school.

After a quick stop at the shops to get some food and drinks, we drive to the bed and breakfast and get there at 4:15 p.m. The entire villa is just for us. My friends Gilda, Laure, and Aurélie, and their families, are already there, and it feels so good to see them and jump into their arms. Laure shows me her baby, Gabriel, now ten months old with crazy blue eyes, her daughter Margaux, a four-and-a-half-year-old with curly hair, and her small doggy, Chance, a white terrier with seven allergies out of the eleven known in dogs. He's Elyze's instant best friend. She loves dogs, and this one is all hers. It's awesome to be with the girls again and so much better for Justin to be able to participate in our conversations, as my friends speak English fluently.

We drink, laugh, talk, cook, and just enjoy our time together. It's so good to be with them again. Friendship is when you realise that even ten years later, you're still the same people. Though husbands and kids have been added to the picture, you remain the same crazy bunch. We're back together in this little house, on top of a hill, in the middle of the French countryside. There's a bedroom for each of our families, with a common kitchen to share our meals and celebrate life and the New Year together. The champagne is flowing on the first night, and we wish for a great and healthy 2017. Then we immortalise the moment with selfies and chat until late. I'm so happy to have my friends by my side again.

The next day, after another *raclette*, we walk through the village of *Villeneuvette*, down south. Jack and Elyze are excited to hold Chance's leash and nearly fight over it. I'm with all of my friends, and it warms my heart. It feels so good to walk in the countryside, the kids running around us, talking about life, our families, and work, as if we've all lived in the same town since forever. I love them so much and miss them. I wish we could live together in the same country, if not in the same city.

That night, we have a big laugh about a business project we could do together in Australia and how it would be cool to work together again. We have the cancer talk as well, but it's easy with them. It's hopeful, honest, and concerned, with no false hope and no fake wishes. Just a raw and genuine conversation. With them, I can joke about my death. I can be sarcastic, and they help me laugh about it. That's a real friendship to me. They're my friends, and I love them more than they could ever imagine. They offer me a lovely silver bracelet with an angel on it, as a reminder of them being my guardian angels. It's the most beautiful present I've received from anyone other than my husband. They move me and are so good to me.

On our last day, it's hard to say our goodbyes, as I'm not sure if I will ever see them again, and I'm extremely saddened by the situation. We've had such a fantastic time together in this house, living together for a couple of days. It's been a short but amazing visit.

I'm raising funds for my second Melanoma March, but because people were so generous in helping me with this trip, it's been quite difficult to raise any money, so I'm selling black bracelets labelled with *Hope for melanoma* for the cause. Before leaving, they don't hesitate one second to buy one each, and I'm in tears.

It's so tough to say goodbye to these three amazing souls. They've given me so much love for the past two days, after all these years apart. They're my friends, and I don't have those back in Sydney. I miss them; I miss my family. I've seen so many of the people I love in a week, it's been overwhelming, and I know why: because I have terminal cancer and because I love them. I don't have much time to visit the country, but I enjoy the company of my friends and family around lunches and dinners, in four different parts of France. There are so many people to see but so little time.

They don't hesitate to hold me tight in their arms and comfort me. I'm so happy and thankful for the special time we've shared together but also sad to leave them. They tell me I live too far away, and they're so damn right. I have a good life in our little house and great melanoma specialists, and my husband makes a decent living; but I feel like there's still a hole growing deep inside me. It's a lack of true and deep friendships like theirs. It's so difficult to develop in Sydney. Everyone has their friends already, usually from childhood, and they either don't need or don't have time for more.

My friends feel for me. They know I'm strong and a good fighter. Though they have trouble comprehending how I'm coping, they know I will do great. The tell me they're thinking about me and sending me good vibes every day, and I'm grateful to have such beautiful friends who are crazy, funny, smart, caring, and loving. I'm lucky to be surrounded by so many wonderful people. I just wish I could bring them all back in my luggage.

We make it to Nice and settle in with my parents, glad to all be back together. My parents welcome us, recovered from their terrible colds.

We spend the third day of the year in Italy. It's great to have lunch on the sunny terrace of a nice pizzeria in San Remo, an hour away from my hometown. I'm excited to show Justin how great it is to escape the country just for a day. We also do some shopping and walk around the small town centre. The same evening, my parents are happy to keep the kids while Justin and I enjoy a dinner with my childhood friends. We have so much fun. Some of them couldn't make it for lunch last time, so it's good to see them.

After a fantastic evening at the restaurant, we go for some drinks in Old Nice. We talk, laugh, joke, and relax all night until three in the morning. We don't want to stop the party, but all the pubs are now closed. I'm tipsy, but Justin is drunk after many shots taken straight with my friends Gaétan and Hervé. It's the third time in nearly six years I've seen him like that. The first two times, he was funny, but this time, he falls into tears at the entrance of my parent's building.

"I'm so sorry," he mumbles. "I try so hard to make you happy, but I feel like it's never good enough. I don't know what to do anymore."

"Oh, Justin," I say. "I'm sorry you feel that way. I don't want you to cry. You make me happy, it's just that I feel overwhelmed doing everything at home and with the kids. Taking care of them full time is so hard. I never have a minute for myself, because I'm taking care of everyone else."

"But I try to help you with the kids, too. I'm doing my best, really, but I'm never good enough." This is a lament I've heard often.

"You are good enough. That's why I know that you can do even better. And it's not so much about the chores and the kids. What would really make me feel better is to see you happier and less grumpy in general. Since we left Sydney, it seems that you always find something to whine about instead of understanding why we're here. There's a reason behind this trip. I may never be able to come back here again and see my loved ones. I'm sorry you feel that way, but please, if you want to make me happy, try to enjoy yourself."

"But you're always all over me, asking me to do things, and I try so hard."

"I know, love, but the kids are demanding, and I need your help. I can't take care of them by myself. I also need some time with my friends and family. I don't have them back home. I'd like you to appreciate the moment instead of being on your phone all the time. I don't want you to learn the hard way like I did. Life is short. Witness it." I give him a kiss and hug him.

"But I'm not always on my phone..."

"Babe, you go for a smoke every twenty minutes, and you're on your phone the whole time. If I knew this would be the case, I would have bought the French sim card for my phone, not yours."

"Oh, come on. No one speaks English, and it's hard for me here." Now I can tell he's getting upset.

"Look, you're drunk, and it's late. We should go to sleep. I don't want to argue again. Thank you for your efforts, love, I appreciate it.

But please, just try to be happy and a bit more present for us, that's all," I say as I open the door.

We just don't have the same perspective on things anymore. A death sentence is tearing us apart, not because I'm dying, but because I'm appreciating life so much, and it's painful to see him unhappy. I can't come up with excuses anymore. He's alive and must enjoy life mindfully. He doesn't know how long it will last and should trust me on this one. Instead, it's like he's mocking me, wasting his time on his phone instead of being with his family. He doesn't get that he needs to be actively present in the moment. He spends the next day hungover. I sleep three hours and take care of the kids all day. That evening, my dad organises a dinner with a couple of their friends and my uncle Gérard. They've all known me since I was born and are close to me. Yet, they avoid the cancer subject. Even my uncle who lost his wife, my dad's sister, to breast cancer.

My friends were able to talk to me about it. The raw facts of the disease, the treatments, and how to deal with your own death, along with the uncertainty of the future. I've never felt uncomfortable with them, but I'm uncomfortable now. They're talking to me about insignificant stuff, and I feel like they awkwardly avoid the subject. Maybe they think I've had enough of discussing it.

After dinner, I sell them my bracelet to raise funds for the march, which forces them to talk about it. Just a little, though. They try to stay positive. And again, they tell me that of course I will survive. I'm upset but feel for them at the same time, because it's probably hard to deal with the reality of the situation. I guess with some people it's difficult for me to be raw and honest. I have a hard time telling them they don't have to tiptoe around the subject and can ask me anything, so I downplay it, not wanting to hurt or bother them. I pick and choose who I tell and try to understand that some people just don't know what to say.

On our last day in Nice, we visit the biggest park in town, Park Phoenix. It has beautiful fauna and flora, and the four of us have lots of fun together.

It's the first week of January, and already it's time to leave France and kiss my parents goodbye. We have another flight, this time to New York, with a quick transfer in Zurich. Fifteen hours of flying, and it goes pretty well. The kids are so tired from all these visits and moving around, they sleep pretty much all the way. So do we.

The previous night, we had a hard time figuring out how we would go from the airport to our hotel, but we finally found a chauffeur service. The driver comes with a massive black van, and I feel like we're a VIP band, except we have six suitcases and a stroller instead of instruments.

Jack and Elyze have been awake for a little while since we left the plane, and Jack runs around like crazy while waiting to pass the border. It's hard to catch him. We've prolonged the day by an extra six hours with the time difference, and we're all overtired. But I'm excited already. I can't wait to see the Big Apple.

We put the kids in their seats and drive to Times Square, where the Sheraton hotel is located. Our driver comments on the itinerary, and it's pretty cool to have some information about where to eat and what to do or avoid from a local.

When we get to the hotel, I buy some yummy hot dogs and Philly cheese dogs from one of the mobile snack vendors around the block, while Justin brings the kids upstairs. Back in our tiny room, I unpack the only luggage we have for the next few days and put everything in the drawers and cupboard. It's lucky I've already packed the stuff we don't need into the other bags, because there's not much space to move around. Then we all crash into a deep sleep.

The next day when I wake up and open the blinds, I discover a great view of the city centre and the buildings surrounding us. One of them displays the time and temperature, and I'm shocked to read it's negative twelve degrees Celsius at eight in the morning. I knew it would be cold, but come on. I pack a big bag for all the jackets, beanies and scarves, so we can finish dressing downstairs in the hotel lobby.

The kids are already rugged up in four layers of clothing, and when we add their beanies, jackets, and hoodies on top, Elyze can't bring her hands together. We put them in the pram and add blankets and a rain cover. After more than forty minutes of preparation, we're ready to face the freezing-cold New York weather. I want to take the ferry to the Statue of Liberty, but as we walk outside, we feel some light moisture falling on our faces…it's snowflakes.

Change of plans. We're going to Central Park, as I've always wanted to see it under a blanket of snow. It's too bad we can't do the carriage with horses, as there's definitely no room for a pram. As we walk, Jack leads the way, standing in his pram, facing forward, his body only protected by the back of his seat. He doesn't want to wear his gloves or the blanket. His jacket is super warm, but I'm afraid he's going to get cold.

We discover all the beautiful landmarks: the rink, the Alice in Wonderland sculpture, the Bethesda fountain, the lake, and the mall. It's mesmerising. There are only a few crazy people jogging, and us. There are no tracks in the snow yet, and old street lamps and bridges offer a stunning landscape. We can't make out the buildings surrounding the park, as we can barely see ten metres away now. The light snowflakes have quickly changed into a snowstorm, and the wind beats our faces. The walk pushing the pram gets harder as the snow accumulates on the ground, so we decide to leave the park after seeing the Cleopatra needle, by an exit on 5th Avenue.

It's weird to be here, after seeing all the movies and TV shows featuring New York. I'm walking these streets, realising another dream of mine, even if it means fighting the snow and the lowest temperatures I've ever experienced.

We head to Columbus Circle, a massive shopping centre, in order to find refuge. The weather is now painful to cope with, and our cheeks and eyes are burning from the cold. Who can live in such weather conditions? The empty bag is quickly filled with all our layers of clothing, and we enjoy a meal in the warmth.

We have lunch in a sort of grocery store where we can buy any kind of food. The prices are based on weight. We also get a large coffee, and I confirm what everyone has told me, which is that coffee definitely sucks in the United States.

After a walk in the galleries, the kids play mannequins in the windows of the shops, and we put back on all our layers of clothes before going back into the cold. We head to Nike Town, an entire building dedicated to the sports brand, with six levels of apparel and shoes. Too bad for me, there are no discounts. I was hoping that after Christmas sales would be on, but I guess it's NYC, and obviously with tourists, sales are pointless. We still look around while Jack is perched on the mannequin's pods, dancing to the background music, to the amusement of the staff. We leave empty-handed and walk back to the hotel for a warm bath and another Philly cheese steak. I love it.

After all this snow, we're lucky to have a beautiful sunny sky the next morning. It's still freezing cold, but at least we don't have to fight a storm and are glad to be able to walk around the street peacefully. On the right corner block of our hotel, there's a Wendy's diner where we enjoy a massive, and expensive, breakfast of blueberry pancakes for the babies and chocolate ones and coffee for us. I ask for a refill of my black coffee, and I feel like we're in the movies.

With the leftovers now in a doggy bag, we have enough to munch on for the rest of the day. We walk down to Times Square, past Bryant Park and the public library, to reach the Empire State Building and nearly miss the entrance. Going through a security check with a pram and both sleeping babies is quite a challenge, but we finally reach the top.

The view is amazing, but it's so freaking cold that I struggle to take photos. My hands are freezing in seconds when I remove them from my gloves. I take pictures around the top deck and run back inside to contemplate the view from behind the windows. Justin takes over, and I keep the kids inside while he also goes for a quick look around. The view is magical with all the snow on the rooftops, but I don't even think of looking at Central Park. I'm so cold, my brain doesn't work properly. I just stare at the city skyline. But we do manage to capture it in pictures.

Then we walk to Grand Central and admire the beauty of the train station. Again, I recall all the movies I've seen featuring this magnificent place, and I'm glad to be here with my little family. It's grandiose. We stay for a little while in the middle of the station, looking around at the beautiful architecture, surrounded by stairs, lights, an amazing ceiling painted with constellations, the American flag, and the old ticket offices.

After a quick picture with the nicest cops we've seen in the U.S. so far, we have a coffee in a sort of food court on the side of the main concourse and leave the building to walk to Times Square. The kids have been pretty good all day, and I'm stunned they've stayed so long in the pram without too much fuss. They love to visit and look around, discovering new places. They definitely take after me.

We're amazed to walk through Times Square with hundreds of lit-up advertising screens. It's astonishing. I imagine all the people who were probably here for New Year's Eve a week ago, watching the countdown. We take a picture while the snow falls again and walk undercover for some crazy shopping at M&M's World. I must have the giant mugs featuring Yellow and Red, a nightie, and a lanyard. I get a couple of tees for Justin and some blankets for the kids, and we're out of the three-level building of one of my favourite confectionery brands.

It's our last day in town. Time flies when you're having fun, and we are. I go for more shopping at the Levi's Store in Times Square. Prices are usually mad, so it would be silly not to take advantage of the half-price sale. We get two pairs of jeans, three tops, a belt, and two track pants. It's with two monster bags that we're going to spend the day out.

We take the metro in Times Square to Little Italy, where we all eat two beautiful wood fire pizzas. Then we go to a Chinese bakery in Chinatown before walking through the City Hall District, where I'm glad I get to see the court where they film the series *Law and Order*. From there we head to the Brooklyn Bridge. Jack and Elyze are asleep by then, so Justin and I can really savour the moment together. We take some selfies and pictures of the beautiful bridge and its views. From there, we can see the other bridge on the Hudson River, the City Hall District, and One World. The architecture of the bridge, with all the ropes and wood flooring, is stunning. I love it.

After walking across the 9/11 Memorial and Museum, and imagining the chaos it must have been on that day, we head to Battery Park to take the free ferry to Staten Island. Jack plays with a squirrel and doesn't want to leave the little guy, but we manage to get to the terminal where hundreds of people are waiting. It's impressive to see everyone embarking onto the boat, and once on board, Jack and Elyze have a lot of fun. Another transport added to their collection. The Statue of Liberty seems quite small from the ferry windows but still bigger than the one in Paris. I also notice that her little island is quite far away from the city.

Once we see it, we go straight back onto the return ferry to the city and witness an amazing sunset of orange and pink, reflected on the city skyline buildings. It's night time when we get off the boat, and we quickly drop by Wall Street before taking the metro back to Times Square to enjoy our last dinner in New York at Applebee's, a famous pub. There, we have massive cocktails, kids' meals, a burger for Justin, and mac 'n' cheese for me. There was no way I was going to leave the U.S. without trying this dish. We admire the lights of Time Square one last time before our last night in the city that never sleeps.

The last morning, I finish packing our stuff, and we walk around the block to see Rockefeller Center. It's lucky we saw the gigantic tree here a couple of days ago, because now it's gone. When we come across the Lego Land store, we decide to enter due to pure curiosity, and wind up spending two hours in there. They have this gigantic Lego sculpture of the Rockefeller Center and a spy game associated with it. Justin and I had to find all the enigmas, including Batman, and all the dogs, bicycles, cameras, and famous characters. We get rewarded with three little characters we can create ourselves, and a Batman set.

Jack and Elyze walk around, playing with everything they can touch, and it's tough to get through all the little heads, bodies, and accessories displayed in small boxes while looking after the kids, but we have a great time. After our last hot dog, our driver picks us up at the hotel at 1:30 for our last transfer to the airport to catch our six-p.m. flight.

We're pretty happy to be going back home after such a big trip around the world with our two babies. It's been exhausting, but I'm glad I had the chance to see all my friends and family, the people I love, my country, my hometown, and discover a city I've only dreamed of for so long. From now on, when I watch a movie filmed in New York, it won't be the same anymore. It will remind me of this magical trip.

19

We're back in Sydney, and Justin and I have a week off together. But what's supposed to be a great romantic week ends up being a dreadful time for us. I have scans and doctor appointments three out of the five days, and Justin doesn't really want to waste his time going with me.

He finally comes for the PET scan, and I leave him in the waiting room once the doctor calls me. While lying in the radiation room for an hour, I update him via text messages to let him know what time I should be out and also that my phone is running out of battery. When I come out two hours later after a crappy time of radioactivity loneliness, he isn't there or at the car. Without any cell phone, I have to go back inside the hospital and ask the lady at reception to call him, only to find out that he's at the car. I'm disappointed and heartbroken. He knows these scans make me anxious, and I'd been hoping to be able to hold his hand when it was over and have him ask me how I'm feeling while walking me to the car. Instead, we argue on the drive home.

"Where were you?" I ask, upset.

"I was at the car."

"No, you weren't. I came out as soon as I was done." I'm furious.

"I was, but then I saw this lady who had a flat tyre and helped her change it."

"Well, that's very nice of you, but I also needed your help, and you weren't there. I sent you text messages to update you up until thirty minutes before I was out, so you knew when to come back. At least you could have notified the front desk, so they could tell me what was happening." I'm saddened. I need his support, and I don't feel he understands. I miss my friends so badly now.

"I didn't want to wait two hours there, okay? And I don't know. I thought you would come to the car anyway," he yells back at me.

"But I needed you, so we could walk to the car together, and you could support me. You know how hard these scans are for me. What's the point of you coming along if you're not there once I'm out? I don't need a driver. I want my husband by my side. Do you know how bad I felt not seeing you? And with my phone being dead, I couldn't reach you."

"Okay, all right… Enough!" he shouts and shuts himself down.

"You know, if you don't want to be here for me, you don't have to. You don't have to come with me tomorrow for my CT and my MRI. I can drive myself, like I usually do. I don't want to share my stupid cancer journey with you anymore. If it's just going to make me feel worse with you than without you, I'd rather do it without you. That way, you won't waste your time driving me."

He doesn't insist on coming the next day, which breaks my heart. I was hoping he would jump in the car without asking. Of course, I would be happy to have his support. Though I'd always thought our love was enough to see us through, sometimes I have my doubts. We need so much more to make it work. I'm also pissed off, because he seemed grumpy on our trip overseas. I don't know what it was about. He did mention not being able to speak the language, but I think it was more than that. Maybe it was because he couldn't handle the kids full time or the small space we had to share with my parents, and not to mention the cold, the snow, the constant changing of planes, and the jet lag.

At some point, I'd thought about going by myself, but I really wanted to introduce Justin and the kids to my friends and family. I just wish he would have understood the importance of the trip. It wasn't constantly terrible, but the overall feeling was that he wasn't happy, and I felt guilty about it. For once, it was all about me, but he should have also made an effort. We don't go back often, and I may never go back at all. I live in his country without my friends or family. I wish he could put himself in my shoes sometimes. But even if he did, he wouldn't comprehend what I'm missing, as he doesn't care to have any friends, and he comes from a family that isn't supportive or reliable.

I'm sad and lonely, already missing the emotional support, so I take it out on my partner. I'm sorry he wasn't as excited as I was. I'm heartbroken he's dodgy in supporting me through this, but I still love him, and I want to believe that we just have to improve our communication skills in order to get through the rough times. I'm sure we can be a better team. I may not be here forever, and I wish we could savour the moments we have together as much as we can.

Finally, Justin comes with me to discuss the results of my scans the following day, and they're great. I'm still NED, so even if the tumours are still present, there's no activity on the PET scan. I will have scans every three months from now on. Who knows how long this can go on for? I hope a lifetime, but my oncologist seems pretty stunned by these results. However, it still stresses me out that the longer I go without a safety net, the more chance there is of the cancer coming back.

Again, I decide to use the next three months to finish all the family photo books, exercise even more, and plan my next move. I want to have some kind of activity and may even go back to work. Having cancer is challenging enough on our marriage, and financial pressure is definitely not helping us. But it would put more pressure on us to take care of the kids and the house, and I'd require more help at home from Justin after a full day of work.

I want to assist my family financially but avoid the stress, I'm just not quite sure how. I've always wanted to be my own boss, but starting my own business would be a huge undertaking and won't help with the finances, so I'm thinking about going back to my previous job. If my next scan is okay, I will. For now, I need to finalise everything I've started.

We have a barbecue with Jack and Elyze for Australia Day. Jack gets sick that night and doesn't sleep for two nights in a row, and of course, I'm in charge, so I try to sleep in to recover. But Justin doesn't accept it, because he works during the week, and I don't. So we argue again. Not long this time, because I'm tired of it.

I don't say anything when the kids are still in their pyjamas at ten a.m. and haven't eaten breakfast. Nothing is planned for lunch, and the dishwasher is still full of clean dishes. Every Saturday morning I'd mention all the things he could help me with, but this time I don't. I just dress up the kids and feed them. Then I play with them and prepare lunch. I barely have the time to sit for a coffee. Sometimes I wonder why I sleep in if I just wind up running around like a chicken with its head cut off as soon as I'm awake.

In the afternoon, I take the kids outside in our backyard to play in the little above-ground pool we bought before Australia Day.

But Justin remains inside, playing games with guns on his Xbox that I don't want the kids to see. After an hour, I have to remind him that he has a family playing outside, and he finally joins us, forced and resigned.

By the end of the day, he packs a bag and leaves without explanation, just saying that he's tired of being treated like crap. I don't feel like a princess, either. I'm more like Cinderella these days, before meeting Prince Charming. I don't know what to think anymore. Am I falling out of love? I'm not really proud of him anymore. There have been too many unresolved arguments slept on and too many mornings pretending nothing happened the night before. I'm tired. Now that my cancer is stable, I'm wondering how I want to spend the rest of my life. Justin is a great father, but I feel like it's hard for him to also be a great partner.

This awful cancer affects my mood, and it's always in the back of my mind, putting a sort of veil over my happiness. It's like all the light in the world is filtered through it, and I'm unable to see things the way I used to. Or maybe I'm looking through special glasses. My vision has been changed forever. But I don't want it to be for the worse. I want to make the most out of these new glasses, since I can't live without them anymore. I have a sword over my head that can drop at any time. I'm subject to a death sentence, wondering what I've done wrong. It's unfair.

Justin isn't a bad man. He works hard, even if he doesn't seem to like his job anymore. And he's a good-hearted man, but I always feel like a nagging wife with him. He never says anything nice to me anymore and never apologises when he's rude, yells at me, or calls me names. He also doesn't thank me for all the hard work I do in the house and with the kids. Our mutual respect is on the road to extinction. The four legs of any relationship stool—pride, respect, desire, and love—are falling apart, and we're going down. I'm not sure how I can save us anymore, but I know I want to. They say cancer either brings you closer or tears you apart. Once again, I'm afraid we're the worst-case scenario.

From day one, I knew this relationship would be challenging. We come from different backgrounds, have different beliefs, and are from different countries. But we had the same values, hopes, and expectations of the life we wanted to have together. I also had faith in him, since he left everything to follow me in my picking quest and had quit smoking for me. He left his bachelor way of life and cared for me like no other man has ever cared for me before. But now I feel ripped off, because if

I'd known he would rather spend time on his Xbox or on his phone than with his family, I'm not sure I would have married him.

The night before he left, I told him that I was deeply saddened about our relationship situation lately, and he replied with something along the lines of, "Whatever you want." For real? It didn't even make sense. And my heart broke. Mister *"I don't care"* demonstrating once again that he isn't the man I fell in love with anymore. And the worst part is that it starts to open my eyes to everything else.

Since he left, I haven't cried. Like, my eyes are dried after all the tears I've had the past six years, I can't find any left. He texts me the next day, and even though I don't want to answer—because he always tries to solve our conflicts by text messages, and I hate it—I do.

All these chores I'm doing by myself, and all the things I have to ask him to do in order for them to be done, is like I'm talking to my teenage son. He even has the guts to say that it's normal for me to do it all, because I'm not working. But even when I did work, it was the same. I was doing it all back then, too. He can pretend that he's doing his best, but it's not enough for me. It's not that he isn't good enough but that he isn't helping enough.

To top it all off, there's all of his whining and swearing, and the fact that he never talks to me about anything deep, important, and interesting, unless I bring up the subject. Even the election of the U.S. president caused arguments. Justin thought that because it was the Americans' decision, it didn't affect us. In an interconnected world of globalisation? Really? Of course, we have to be worried about the silly decisions this rude guy makes. But again, he took out the *"I don't care"* card.

I'm so over him not caring for anything, not even me or my feelings. I used to get hurt, but since he left, I'm numb. Of course I'm upset that our relationship has issues, but I'm not sure I'm sad to lose him. Sometimes I feel like he's just waiting for me to die, so then he won't have to deal with me anymore. It's horrible to feel that way. No wonder I'm not happy. But I'm not sure what will bring me happiness anymore, except for my kids. They are my world. My happy bubble, my pride, and the best reason I have to stay alive.

Justin comes home every night for the next four nights, but he won't say anything. He stands there looking at me feeding and bathing the kids and doesn't even help. I tell him I need time to think about us, about our lives, and find some kind of miracle solution for us to be a happier couple, and that unless we come up with a solution, it's pointless for him to come back. I don't want to talk about our issues in front of the kids, either, as it ends with arguments and him yelling at me with either, "Okay, all right," or "I'm not good enough anyway. You'd better find someone else."

On the third night, he comes with six red roses and says, "Just to say I'm sorry and stuff." Then he adds, "I love you. Tell the kids I love them, too" and he leaves after taking something he needed in his shed and the mail in the letterbox. It's nice, but this isn't enough. It's too easy. No discussion at all. He pretty much wasted a bunch of flowers, then. He should have developed his apologies. "Stuff" isn't the best problem-solver, and I actually find it disrespectful, like he was forced to apologise. Is this all I deserve? All we're worthy of?

He finally comes back the next day, and we have a heated conversation about him helping me with not only what I tell him to do, but also to think about what needs to be done. Because the mental load is often the problem, not the actual tasks. It doesn't help. He's still yelling, and I don't want to be yelled at, so I leave to pick up the kids at day care. I think he will leave again, but he's there when I come back and tells me, "I will do whatever it takes. Even if I'm not happy about it, just ask me."

I do it, but I hate asking. That's what makes me feel like a nagging wife.

Since then, I've done lots of thinking. After being overwhelmed with so much love and support from my family and friends during our big trip, I guess it's been hard for me to come back to the harsh reality of my loneliness here. I have a few mates but no one I can really rely on, except for Justin. This simple thought is depressing. But living in France is out of the question, since he doesn't speak the language, so I have to deal with it and make the most out of my days here from now on.

Justin isn't perfect, and yes, I have to tell him everything I want him to help me with, but he's trying his best—his real best— to assist me with the kids and the house. I can tell he's making an effort, and that's all that matters to me.

Okay, I'm still waiting for us to get some quality romantic time, but without reliable babysitters, it's tough. Our marriage has been through so much in only six years, and we got married after knowing each other for only a few months. Yet we're still here, working hard on our relationship, going through life together without much family support. We've endured the loss of our first unborn child, the arrival of a thirty-week premature baby, and terminal cancer. Some couples don't go through half of these issues in twenty years. Life is hectic, and we may doubt sometimes, but our love has been intensified, and our faith in each other keeps growing stronger. We just need to work through these overwhelming times.

And now that my health is getting better, we want to enjoy our new "normal," worry less about what the future holds for us, and embrace the few happy times we can get out of our busy young parents life. I'm hoping I will stay healthy for many years and defy the odds until I die in my sleep, my hair white and my skin wrinkly, holding my husband's hand.

By the end of February, I tick another item off my bucket list: I get a cover-up tattoo for the tribal butterfly and Chinese love sign I've had on my left shoulder blade since I was eighteen, that Justin hated. After about fourteen hours of suffering, I have a colourful tattoo representing an angel wing embracing a hibiscus and two frangipani flowers—a symbol of femininity and strength—with a black feather in a ribbon shape that ends in flying birds and the names of my kids above it all. I'm quite happy with the results and glad to have my children literally under my skin.

I've also finished the birthday letters and the first two photo books for 2016. I will need a third one, as it's been a captivating year, full of events. After these books, I will have to find out what my next step will be. I'd like to see my kids more often, but I have to figure out if I will go back to work first. I don't feel comfortable not knowing what will happen with my health into the future. It's difficult to make a decision. I don't really want to go back to my insensitive boss, and I'm not sure if returning to work will affect negatively on my health, because of the stress and pressure. Uncertainty doesn't help the decision-making process. Trying to anticipate what could happen, and going from planning the end of the road to finally living in the future, makes surviving cancer an anxious and heart-wrenching journey.

20

It's April 2017. I'm starved for comfort and anxious. Surviving is exhausting and emotionally draining. I've spent eighteen months watching the Internet for melanoma research articles, new treatments, and also other patients' stories. I've seen so many people dying around me. Too many. Every couple of days, someone receives bad results or dies of melanoma. It's devastating, and I can't help but think that I could be next. A twenty-five-year-old woman had melanoma in Queensland and wrote a successful blog. I asked her what kind of treatment she was on back when I was diagnosed. Ever since, I've been following her journey from a distance. Anna, my nurse, had told me not to get too close and avoid this kind of social media activity, as it could depress me quickly, and she was right. I've had to remove myself from a lot of groups, because at some point it's overwhelming and increases the negative thoughts in my head. But when I learn that this particular girl passed away after two years of fighting the disease, it hurts more than ever.

I knew it would happen eventually, but having seen her posts for the past two years, like all of us, I thought she had some more fight left in her. But her time was up. She didn't have any treatment options left, and she was gone in a couple of months. Just like that. Again, when treatment options are out, you go fast. That's also the reason why I've done my boxes, the cards, the photo albums, and planned my funeral—all of it, just to avoid wasting my remaining time, when I'd like to cuddle my kids and my husband instead. Since she passed away, I feel like I'm slipping down my fragile thread of life, but I'm still trying to holding on to all my strength and hopes. I do everything I can to keep focused and remember that I'm lucky to be where I am today as I slowly climb back up on the thread. Staying on top of it helps, because if I have to slip again, I won't fall. My arms are getting sore, and it's harder when I lose energy and cry, letting out my fears and sadness. But I'm not at the end of it... not yet.

It's always difficult for me when one of my melanoma mates dies. It makes my mortality even more real. When they fall like flies, I get scared. I feel closer to my own death. It's a constant reminder of my disease, of the danger of my condition, and it usually occurs just when I start to get comfortable in my new "normal" life. I'm hoping that the more positive and mindfully I live, the more chance I'll have to survive and strengthen the thread, so the sword hanging over me never cuts my neck.

I've been so lucky. I have it easy compared to so many. The worst side-effects I've had were extreme fevers and joint pain. But it's now been eight months without any treatment, and there's still *no evidence of disease* based on my last PET scan. I'm one of the rare lucky ones, and I intend to stay that way.

I want to rewrite each birthday card, closer to the date, and give them myself, with a kiss. I'm waiting to compose my twenty-first birthday card message. If I don't have much time left to live, I will make sure I do this last one. I'll wait until the cancer is back and I'm not able to get any treatment or clinical trial and run out of options, but I'm hoping that day will never come.

This book is another of my bucket list ticks, and I'm happy to write it. I've also obtained my citizenship, after getting a perfect score on the test. My next step will be to take some time off with the kids and maybe go back to work. I want to help my family again. Also, if I survive ten years, I can't spend that time not doing anything. It would drive me crazy. Meanwhile, I'm spending my days writing or going to the doctors.

I book an appointment with a private ears, nose, and throat specialist for Jack, as I'm not waiting for September. He's been waking up every night now, telling me he's choking, and having tonsillitis monthly. I want his tonsils and adenoids removed ASAP.

I enjoy playing with my babies, of course. Elyze wants to use the potty already, and they're growing so fast. Jack is definitely not developing enough, as people think they're twins. I can't wait for him to get better and finally thrive. Elyze also talks a lot more and is definitely a smart cookie. Jack is about to go to pre-school. He's naughty and cheeky, the typical *threenager*… and they love each other so much. I'm a happy mother, and I love my family. I'm living an emotional roller coaster, but I'm lucky.

My oncologist has reassured me that the more time I spend without active tumours, the more chance I have of surviving longer. And that changed everything. Before, I used to think the opposite; that the longer I stayed out of treatment, the more chance I had of getting the cancer back. But I was wrong. Dealing with surviving has been tough emotionally, but I'm stable, and somehow my immune system took over and is fighting efficiently against the black beast. It apparently happens to a handful of people, but usually the cancer comes back after three months for 50 percent of them. The other two and a half fingers are like me… lucky bitches. I'm a freaking miracle.

Since they told me that, I feel like I can live a "normal" life again. I'm not worried as much anymore. Of course, cancer will always be in the back of my mind, as long as there's no cure for it, but I'm not scared of dying on a daily basis anymore. I feel free for the first time in the last nineteen months. I'm not as stressed as I used to be, thinking that every little pain in my body is the cancer coming back. And I'm feeling pretty good for the first time in what feels like a very, very long time. My last results show a new uptick of activity in my lymph node, but my oncologist doesn't think it's cancer, so I will have to do another PET scan in a couple of months. Meanwhile, I'm socialising again and found a nice group of expatriate mums living in my area to go out and about with. It's just what I needed.

I'm thinking it could be a lifetime thing. I could live like any other person on Earth. I can go back to work. But I won't forget that I must live my life like I will be hit by a car tomorrow, with no regrets, to the fullest. Since I've had cancer, I can see clearly for the first time in my life. I have terrible vision and require glasses, but I can make out the details and the depth of everything like never before. I was blind and now I see. Life is beautiful, in poverty or wealth, in health or sickness. Trust me, I've experienced all of it, to a certain extent.

But where life is even more beautiful is in love. It helps me fill my anger and desperation void with peace and hope. The love for my family gives me wings to fight, and I hope I will remain a freaking miracle, keeping this cancer away from me. Terminal is my condition, but my life is far from over. And somehow, through pain and anger, my husband and I have become better at communicating and helping each other. He's doing so much now at home and with our children; I'm sure that he would be better at supporting me emotionally if the black beast comes back. Our bond is stronger than ever, and we're hopeful for our future.

The hardest part of cancer is really the emotional journey. It's been a lonely one. When I first told people, I was overwhelmed by the support and attention. They'd bring me pasta and offer their help. But after a few months, no one came around anymore or offered help. I felt lonely and misunderstood, even by my family and friends. At times I actually wondered if people were waiting for me to die. And because I wasn't, they were keeping quiet, forgetting I was still there.

I wasn't breaking news anymore. People like drama. It was like because I was surviving and had a better outcome than expected, I wasn't worthy of love and attention anymore. I was in *too-good* shape? I even felt that way with my melanoma mates at the Melanoma March this year. For the first one I was dying, and people cared so much, but when I participated in this one, it was like I wasn't interesting enough because I was NED with no treatment. I can't believe the nature of humans. A story of hope isn't better than a story of death? I was shocked and saddened.

I still need emotional support. Who knows how long I will stay in such a good position? But like my best friend, Justin, says, "The most important thing is that you have more time, and too bad if they're not happy about it." Because on top of everything, I feel guilty that I'm surviving with no treatment, and they aren't. I have another chance at life that I don't want to waste, and sometimes it's overwhelming. But somewhere, I lost my place in the "normal" people society, and it doesn't seem like I have one in the "cancer patients" one, either. I'm like an outcast, and that makes me feel even lonelier. I guess everybody thinks that because my life looks ordinary again, they don't need to be there for me anymore. But they don't realise that normal is over.

I feel like I have to live by my values and respect the honour I've been given, otherwise I may lose my health again, and my life along with it. It's like I have to prove to whoever is in charge upstairs that I deserve to live somehow.

I've changed. I've became more humble and maybe more cautious of what I'm doing and why I'm doing it, for sure. I expect even more from myself, and I feel like I owe my life, so I want to make sure I'm not screwing with *karma*. I've done pretty well so far and managed to get all the things I've ever wanted. I'm blessed with my guardian angel, my Grandma Denise, who's watching over me, and I don't want to disappoint her. I'm still adjusting to the new version of myself, but it's a better version, for sure. Karine 2.0 is now operational, and I'll try not to crash again, because I don't really want to go through another reboot. I feel like my entire life was a succession of cycles. I have so many stories. I've been re-born again and again, but this time it's different. It wasn't my choice. I'm lucky to be where I am today, because I'm free.

I have this sensation that the nightmare is over. I know it can come back at any time, but for now, it's not there. Living in the present is okay for me. I can live my life mindfully. At the moment, I'm enjoying a blue sky and a happy life with my beautiful family. We left the umbrellas at home. We have our hats and sunscreen on and are enjoying the warmth of a sunny sky, playing together in our backyard. Rain may come, but not now. Today is beautiful.

21

I spend the entire month of May wondering if I'm ready to go back to work. I don't really want to start a new position, because I may feel overwhelmed trying to prove myself, and I'm not sure I can afford it health-wise. I want to help provide for my family, since I'm healthier and hoping to stay that way for a long time. Maybe going back into my former brand manager role would give me the opportunity to return to an active life without too much pressure, as I've been in this role for so long.

So when June comes, I decide to catch up with my former manager to figure out if we can agree on new working conditions. I don't want to go back full time. I need a better work/life balance. Being with my family remains my priority.

We discuss what's happened to me over the past twenty months, and I know that if I want to be able to work with him again, I have to start with a clean slate. I tell him how I feel about his lack of contact while I was on sick leave, despite the hard work I achieved for so many years, but he brushes it off and asks me to come back the next month.

I will have Fridays off, so I can see my children. He seems genuinely enthusiastic about working with me again, and I understand why when he tells me that I have to manage three brands and two divisions, which is more than when I left. The projects are great, but it means lots of pressuring deadlines, too.

I'm excited to move on but a bit scared, because I know how hard I used to work.

Monday July, third, is my first day back at work. I'm glad to put on my nicest suit and be a businesswoman again. When I enter the building, it feels like nothing has changed. The same receptionist welcomes me with a smile and a quick chat, and I walk upstairs to the same kitchen to make myself an expresso. It feels like I've just woken up from a long and deadly nightmare. I'm back at the same workplace, in the same office, with the same boss. The only difference is that I have a new assistant. She seems nice and smart. I just hope that the task ahead, and the pressure associated with it, won't affect my health. Meditation and mindfulness help me tremendously on a daily basis, and I feel good for the first time in a very long time.

Working definitely provides a sense of normality and helps me stay sane. Also, time really flies when you have so many responsibilities. But staying busy helps me remain positive and limits the number of negative thoughts going through my mind. I leave my work early enough every day to be able to pick up my kids before 5:30 p.m. and enjoy my time with them even more mindfully. And I love that we can spend our Fridays together. Also, since I've gone back to work, Justin is helping me like never before with the chores and the kids. Now I know he will be fine if I'm gone.

With our extra income, we decide to purchase an investment property. Being an owner was on my bucket list, and now we can make it happen. We can't afford anything in Sydney, so we're still renting where we need to live, but we find a three-bedroom house in a small country town in New South Wales. It will pay itself off, and at least if I have to leave this world, Justin and the kids will have some kind of asset.

I go to my scans and see my oncologist every three months, and each time they tell me that I remain a miracle. I feel like I have a nice break from the disease; a window of freedom and opportunity. I can't forget what happened, but I'm trying to pick up where I left off.

Not long after going back to my old life, I lose two of my Facebook mums and melanoma mates in two weeks. One of them was NED for over a year, and after a re-occurrence in the brain, passed way in less than three months. This happens just as I'm getting comfortable in my "living a normal life" shoes. It looks like once this beast gets you, it's not easy to escape, and it could eventually come back and take you for good. So I try to live to the fullest, because I don't know how long it's going to last. Hopefully forever. I pray for it every single day. May I remain a miracle.

After a few months, it's Christmas again. I have a PET scan in a couple of days, and again *scanxiety* is playing tricks on me. But I think I'll be okay and always keep a positive outlook.

Christmas always comes with its double-sided coin: joy and worries. In every happy moment, there's the quick thought that I need to enjoy it, as it may not last forever. So I embrace every moment of laughter, happiness, cuddles, and even the never-ending bedtime process of trying to put my children to sleep. We decorate the Christmas tree with my now two-year-old daughter and my three-and-a-half-year-old son, and I bribe them as soon as I can to be good, otherwise Santa might not come. Life feels great again.

Another tick I can take off my bucket list: going on a cruise to New Caledonia. We're going on holiday for ten days over Christmas. I can't wait.

I will tick off Vietnam and Cambodia as well. My husband and I haven't spent two weeks alone in very a long time. Since my parents plan to come at the end of next year, I decide to book our flight. I will finally see this amazing part of Asia, and though I have to be patient for this one, I'm sure it will be on of a kind.

Also, since I've been back to work, I realise that if I want to stay healthy and happy, I need to change my lifestyle. More and faster is not the answer for me anymore. The world is becoming an over-productive place with over-consumption and overweight and over-connected people, overstressed by greedy and selfish companies. Why do we do that to ourselves? I'm over it.

I don't want to live this way anymore. I want to get back to what's really essential.

I guess working in marketing doesn't help, especially when I'm been told to do it the old-fashioned way. And I start to wonder if it's what I really want to do now. Going back to my previous life was great, because it allowed me to tick my bucket list and helped me realise that it's not what I want to do for the rest of my life. Everything would be simpler if we all oriented towards our basic needs and maintaining a safe planet. I feel like we're living in a toxic world at pretty much all levels. Nowadays, you pay a fortune for vegetables that don't taste like anything, that are full of pesticides, and for people to look after your kids while you work hard just to pay the bills, without being able to afford a house that you barely live in. Isn't it silly?

I miss my children. I have to work most of my Fridays from home to meet deadlines and deal with emergencies, which is difficult with the kids begging me to get off the phone and defeats the purpose of taking the day off in the first place. This wasn't part of the agreement, and I feel frustrated. I would like to have a better quality of life. We don't need all the things we have. I'm not scared of change anymore. My time is precious, and I don't want to end up on my deathbed regretting that I didn't try to have the life I really want.

I've never lived with regrets, and it won't start now. I don't need to win the lottery. I feel like living in a little house down the coast with a veggie patch and some chickens. It's been a long time since I've felt the need for change without being able to put my finger on it. This has been a slow process of realisation, but now I know what I've been craving all this time: freedom and simplicity. And because my health has been stable for a while, I feel it's a good time for that change. I will only live once, and I don't want to wait for my retirement to give me a chance to live how I really want to. Life is too short, and my dreams aren't too big. I don't need a mansion and a yacht but just to live with the people I love, and have healthy food, water, and clean air.

We leave Sydney on the seventeenth of December, and I'm so glad to embark on our ten-day cruise. Having some time off helps me make a serious decision: I deserve better for myself, and I'm going to quit my job. I'm not sure if it's the way my manager is always bringing me down, that I'm under the pump on a daily basis, or the lack of resources, but I just can't go on anymore. If I have to work that hard, I'd rather do it for myself.

Also, I think I've changed, and I can't simply go back to who I used to be. It's not me anymore. After a week back from holidays, I start 2018 with a resignation letter to my manager. I want to create my own business. I figure that at least if it doesn't work out, I would have tried.

Every time I question how I live, I try to remember what life is all about. I don't want to forget the hard lessons I've learned. My family will always come first. The New Year is here, and it looks like I finally need another reboot. After living, and then surviving, I need one final transformation to thrive in my new life. My motto will stay the same: carpe diem.

Epilogue

2018 has been quite a year for me. Once my health improved, and having a future started to become a reality, I wasn't prepared for it. Having a future meant taking on responsibilities. I realised I couldn't live the way I used to before cancer, nor the one I'd been living since surviving it. I wanted to thrive.

Through my cancer journey, I managed to cope with the roller coaster of emotions and the uncertainty, and became someone else. My values and priorities changed, and I shifted my perspective. I learned to be present and let go. I felt like I was living decently as a caterpillar, introspective in my cancer cocoon. But then I'm transforming into a butterfly, willing to create the best life, using my wings to fly and to thrive.

But the only problem was that I didn't know where to start. Though I knew I wanted to work for myself, I was lost without purpose. Then after much contemplation about a potential online business, I came to the conclusion that it wasn't for me. The ecological impact of my business due to the carbon footprint, wouldn't align with my values.

It took me a couple of months to get to know the new me and what I stood for. Being self-aware and understanding my need for change was crucial. Surviving a death sentence helped me see what was important to me.

Before the disease, I wanted to be a successful businesswoman, high ranked on the corporate ladder, with a six-figure income. But once I realised that I could live again, despite having it all, I wasn't satisfied anymore. The wealth that I was looking for wasn't money, but time and success. It was all about finding happiness and purpose. I wanted balance and fulfilment in my life.

Along with my time, my health also needed to become a valuable commodity, if I wanted to stay alive. Through my research as to how to live a healthier lifestyle, I became minimalist and also discovered my passion for our environment, so I started a zero-waste journey. It allowed me to contribute to a healthier planet by reducing waste to a minimum, and a healthier lifestyle by avoiding processed food, plastics, and chemical exposure. I began with cooking everything from scratch and graduated to creating all of our hygiene products and starting a veggie patch.

Living a simpler life with less "stuff" generated a great feeling of satisfaction and helped me see clearer. But there was still the issue of finding my new career path, while making sure that if I died, I'd have no regrets. If I was going to live a long life, I wanted to enjoy my days doing what I love, while providing for my family. One thing's for sure: I wanted to give back to the community and help people.

As I looked into my past, I remembered how I wanted to become a psychologist after my mum's stroke, but my family had dissuaded me. Later on, while studying communications, I'd thought about becoming a life coach, but it was too new back then, and I wasn't sure I had enough life experience.

But now that I'd been through hell and back, and turned my life around twice, I came to the realisation that I could help any willing person transform their life, as well. All I had to do was remove the mental blocks that create resistance. It didn't matter that I had fifteen years of experience in marketing and a business degree. I could give up my six-figure income and become whatever I wanted, as long as it made me happy.

It was hard for me to think of giving up my comfortable lifestyle, but being satisfied with "good enough" meant never striving to be the best and reaching my true potential. I even called my dad to make sure he'd be okay with my drastic career change, since he'd paid for my business school. I also checked in with my husband, because this would have a huge impact on his life as well. Once I received the support I needed, I went for it. I researched mindset and how to become a life coach. Then I made a decision to invest in myself and spent half of our savings on a full year of learning from amazing mentors and developing my coaching skills.

That's how I found my purpose. Now, I help people to live with no regrets and make their dreams come true. As I like to say, "No dream is too big, no life is too short and it's never too late."

If you wish to contact me, like my Facebook page and/or follow me on Instagram; search for @karinetobin or visit www.karinetobin.com

www.ingramcontent.com/pod-product-compliance
Lightning Source LLC
Chambersburg PA
CBHW031104080526
44587CB00011B/818